Hen Harrier Poems

Lives of British Lizards, Goose and Sons, Norwich, 1970.
Some Effects of Yorkshire Flooding (with J. Radley), Sessions Book Trust, York, 1971.
Pomes and Other Fruit, Headland, Sheffield. 1972.
Adders and Other Worms, Headland, Sheffield, 1972.
Working Seams, North York Poetry, York, 1972.
Bear Skull, North York Poetry, York, 1972. (Revised edition, 1974).
Birches and Other Striplings, Headland, Sheffield. 1973.
Modesty (Swaledale Summer), Headland, Sheffield. 1973.
Pine Marten, Seven Prints, Genera 14, York, 1973.
Horcum and Other Gods, Headland, New Malden, 1975.
Jane in Spain, Genera, Newcastle-upon-Tyne, 1975.
Photosopsis for Basil Bunting, Headland, New Malden, 1975. (2nd ed., 1986).
Rushmore Inhabitation, Blue Cloud Quarterly, Marvin, SD, 1976.
No North Western Passage, Writers' Forum, London, 1976.
Flat Earth, Aloes Books, London, 1976.
Parflèche. Galloping Dog Press, Swansea. 1976.
Otters: Ten Seals, Genera 16, Newcastle-upon-Tyne, 1976.
Voices, The Many Press, London, 1977.
Humility, Spanner, London, 1977.
On Osgodby Cliff, Curlew Press, Harrogate. 1977.
Windscale: Four Cantos, Genera Editions, Newcastle-upon-Tyne, 1978.
Midwinter Housewife, twisted wrist, Hebden Bridge, 1978.
Pentland, Shadowcat, Weardale, 1978.
Some Company (Tea at 40), Genera Editions, Newcastle-upon-Tyne, 1979.
Hunting Bunting, Luksha, New York & San Francisco, 1979.
Ingenuity (Wensleydale Winter), Shadowcat, Weardale, 1979.
Spirits, Shadowcat, Weardale, 1980.
Movement, Pig Press, Durham, 1980.
Time over Tyne: Poems, The Many Press, London, 1980.
A Celebration of the Stones in a Watercourse, Galloping Dog, Newcastle, 1981.
Big Cats, Islamabad, 1988
A Second Book of / Look at Birds, Genera Editions, New York, 1981. (2nd ed. 1989).
Cuddie Cantos, Bellingham, 1986/7 (2nd edition 2000).
Eyes Own Ideas, Pig Press, Durham, 1987.
Luigi Pirandello: Navigator, Shadowcat, Weardale, 1988.
In Afghanistan: Poems 1986-1994, Writers' Forum, London, 1994. (2nd ed. 2001).
Poems to Basil Bunting, Writers' Forum, London, 1994. (2nd ed. 2001).
Shots at Otters, RWC, Reading, 1994.
Goshawk Lives, Form Books, London, 1995.
Bewcastle & Other Poems for Basil Bunting, Vertiz, USA, 1996.
Otters and Martens, Shearsman Books, 2004.
The American Poems, Shearsman Books, 2005.
Gyrfalcon Poems, Shearsman Books, 2007.
Poems from Afghanistan, Shearsman Books, 2013.

COLIN SIMMS

Hen Harrier Poems

Shearsman Books

This first edition published in the United Kingdom in 2015 by
Shearsman Books Ltd, 50 Westons Hill Drive, Emersons Green
BRISTOL BS16 7DF

Shearsman Books Ltd Registered Office (this address not for correspondence)
30–31 St. James Place, Mangotsfield, Bristol BS16 9JB

www.shearsman.com

ISBN 978-1-84861-429-1

ACKNOWLEDGMENTS

Some of the poems in this volume previously appeared, often in earlier versions, in the
following journals: *Angel Exhaust, Fire, Genera, Headland, Northern Democrat, Strath,
River Derwent Frieze* (1974) and *The Yorkshire Derwent*. Some were also broadcast
on Radios KTCY and KRAB (USA), BBC Radio Leeds, and *Look North* (Leeds
and Newcastle-upon-Tyne). Some poems, often in previous forms, also appeared in
publications issued by Cape Clear Bird Observatory, Pig Press (Durham), Many
Press (London), Shadowcat (Weardale).

'Winnowing marsh hawks' (p.19) appeared in a different version in the author's
collection, *The American Poems* (Shearsman Books, 2005).

A range of journals, newsletters and newspapers publishing my notes and papers since
1959, mostly British and attention also from broadcasters, until about 1999, in the
northern hemisphere, especially British and North American. For companionship
and help in the field and for transcribing drafts, named in the texts, but most of all
Margaret Hartley and Alexandra Bowman, Brian and Liz West; in the early days also
(not in the text) Tom Robson, Alan Hardy, Eric and M.J. Wilson. Articles and letters
in the *Yorkshire Gazette, Northumberland Gazette, Hexham Courant, Cumberland
News, Westmorland Gazette*, etc.

For Alexandra Bowman

Contents

9

A Preface

Colin Simms came to stay near here in the hills, and here, several times over recent years to study the hen harriers and merlins, which I was pleased he showed me... just as he was a link between me and the great poet of Northumberland his friend Basil Bunting... He read me some of his preliminary writing and the finished work I was glad to comment on; as I am now to recommend his projected books gathering these poems and other writings, like the one published a few years ago on the marten. As I have said before, he is one of the few poets... writing proper scientific stuff.

'Hugh MacDiarmid' (C.M. Grieve) 1975
Brownshank,
Biggar

Readers of this book, perhaps merely browsers and not readers, will perhaps have picked it up because they have heard of some fuss about harriers, hen harriers, an obscure bird of prey, needing help if they are not to become extinct in England, or Britain, and remain so. Their true status: their numbers here at any given time, a matter of controversy... To readers of this book it may be clear that pessimistic censuses or even estimates of the numbers of hen harriers must be wrong, or the author is crazy or a liar. We are, most or all of us, exposed, dominated by, the mass media's treatment of 'information' in this so-called Information Age. Misinformation is a feature of our age – where political expediency and 'publicity' reign supreme.

Recent springs have seen the spectacle of newspaper appeals for information from the public on sightings of hen harriers. That most people, the vast majority, don't recognise such birds safely seems ignored. 'The birds are coming back from their winter haunts' (they are absent from our hills in winter!). This sort of statement is quite wrong. There are more hen harriers on our hills in winter than in summer...

The RSPB must know this and so what they fed, or feed, the local media has to be propaganda; perhaps hoping' twitchers' and other bird-aware people will concentrate on getting out early in spring to find 'returning' harriers and let the RSPB know about them...

'Early spring' in such places, regions, as the North Pennines, the Border hills, the Yorkshire moors and dales, and the Lake District fells is still winter and the harriers still are yet on winter hunting and winter social behaviour – often well into April or even May in some years. Clear-felled and newly planted new 'forests' up to several years old are often amongst their best hunting grounds, but rarely attractive to bird watchers, or indeed ramblers, in my experience. Most of my harrier watching until nesting (if any!) links such favoured areas with the usual routes they use, prospecting, between them.

Cautiously also, those least-known and least advertised (but still often threatened) havens, their roosts, approached or watched from a distance rather than visited, are sometimes used year after year and I don't just mean 'winter' after winter, for there is often a small but significant presence of non-breeding birds about throughout the 'summer'. I've noticed a tendency for some cock birds in this category to display, at least a little; and this can be confusing especially as some 'genuine' potential breeding cocks display nowadays much less, or noticeably less conspicuously, than their forebears used to – it may be that they have learned that breeding success may have better chances if they keep a low profile.

And we must not suppose that these watchers, 'amateur' or 'professional', who see and mark the remarkable 'sky-writing' displays of the cock bird over or near potential breeding-sites are innocent in the critical matter of some success for the hen harrier at home. Other people watch the watchers watching for harriers, and the information passed about isn't always 'safe', and so the birds aren't. More than once in recent years, and overall some twenty times in sixty years, I've known bird watchers, including established scientists, wittingly or unwittingly betray harrier nest-sites to predators (and not only avian ones – egg collectors and other menaces).

§

§

Before their observations are lost, were lost, much information about harriers was, is, available. In the 'sixties I met Sir Herbert Read, with his long and deep knowledge of (especially) the western part of the Vale of Pickering and its tributary dales, in York and usually on the premises of the Yorkshire Philosophical Society and in the Yorkshire Museum nearby, asking him – as I had in the late 'fifties, for memories of harriers in the Vale in his youth and since. At Muscoates Grange they had been regular in winter over the fields, he couldn't say which harrier. That they nested occasionally in the Vale – he thought in the carr lands – and also about the heads of Farndale just where I'd been directed in 1961 by a landowner there, Richmond Brown. These observations, I'm sure, could be repeated over many landscapes of the North Country. But this is hearsay.

Notoriously the Hen Harrier, and other birds of prey, often afford us glimpses only, before they are gone from sight. 'Out of sight is out of mind'. I find the distant and peripheral vision of many, for example in my evening-classes, 1960s-80s, do not pick them up despite their style... These observations started in the early 'fifties, and a few of the early ones may relate to Montagu's Harrier rather than the Hen Harrier, though I believe I have now eliminated nearly or quite all notes and verses not carefully diagnosed, critically determined, of *Circus cyaneus*. Montagu's Harriers were not rare during the 'fifties and 'sixties especially, in parts of North-east England particularly. I was brought up in a hard school of disciplined ornithologists; a number of them listed in acknowledgements throughout this book, and have my own strict standards.

To some extent, these verses serve another function in reporting the presence of a little-known member of our fauna – as my previous works on Goshawk, Marten, Otter, Gyrfalcon have: a hope is that anyone reading or hearing my works will gain, if only 'accidentally', some useful knowledge of the behaviour, occurrence and distribution of these harriers. But amongst the many aspects hardly touched-on here are 'dog fights' observed, rarely but I think significantly, between hen harriers and buzzards (including Rough-legged Buzzard) and hen harrier and red kites (from introductions) in the North of England since 1970 and especially since the spread of the Common Buzzard and then of the Red Kite. Usually the buzzard or kite has repulsed, but not injured, the harrier. I doubt our so-called 'conservation' lobby has considered this factor in the current scarcity of hen-harriers... even our most-open spaces are limited...

Reginald Wagstaffe, Keeper of Zoology at Liverpool Museums and familiar with the Isle of Man and its recorded ornithology, had more reason to be surprised than I had, whose experience was limited to several visits to the island since 1947*, that no harrier was recorded in the excellent and careful Ralfe's *Birds of the Isle of Man* (1905), and we wondered why this was so. We had both seen Hen Harrier there and could not imagine they had just discovered the place since the 'thirties! Nevertheless, these are my first published observations of harriers there, 'authorities' having rejected earlier ones...

§

* For birds and the spring and autumn migrations (and motorcycle races), for finding merlin nests etc., since 1951 and insect fauna since 1953 (including *Stenobothrus stigmaticus* in the '60s (see Ragge).

'I follow my friend Basil Bunting in believing, from experience, that information is carried best by poetry, verse. We did not, do not, know why; and leave the question, with others: as poets we have enough to do; but we assert this particular advantage of poetry, verse, over prose. Often an originator in the forms of his verse, at other times an adapter of accepted shapes Bunting insisted on the "music" of his work; that it should be *heard*. My work is not poetry on his level but it is something else as new; a fresh genre of natural-history verse-making dealing with experience of a single species; a magnificent but little-known bird of prey surprisingly still frequently seen over a large part of the earth – I have watched it in fourteen countries and a range of habitats – most of them the wide open spaces the hen-harrier graces yet in an increasingly "developed" world.

Cursed by some "critics" for putting-up barriers I've put a few rough notes in better order from those years of Bunting anecdotes and stories; engaged at the time with harriers between the North Tyne and the Border bracken beds in glens, cover at forest-edges I had explored in the 'sixties and 'seventies especially Tarrasdale and the Head in the west to where the gleds hid in the Pentlands in the east and places he wanted to go, Middle" and Cheviot the Simonsides and Wannies, the heads of Coquet "where wild goats might flourish; men least". managed to find one place near enough to the road where I could show him their nest as in Wark Forest, but on untrodden bluff where *Dryas* and *Trientalis* showed their faces to the east in the morning, south at "opening time" "these are the kinds of blooms I like the best" he laughed, back in our rooms, "but do you suppose, if we had stayed, they'd have known when to close? Children at the table, he'd indulge in a mime of mother harrier preparing prey for food, tearing and offering pieces to each of her brood (several usually, like ours at "Striding Edge") "Grub up," shouted Basil, cutting each wedge of beef plate pie while I ladle gravy and greens. We'd marvelled at their wavy flight to their nests, "their mates keeping cavey".

§

Winnowing marsh hawks   cleave air   don't push it aside   under
rounding-up ringing over migrating sandhill cranes   high, ablaze on
     mornings haze
nor, with the eagled and thunderbirds   are they tempted   to ride thunder,
when they come to a merging with the place where fables start, the
     fluttering heart
where the white one comes-on Godlike   they'll be seen as the 'best of all'
the better to learn aerodynamics from than the flattering, the tables of
     Lilienthal.
With the ease to rehearse the spring for meadowlarks and all the buzzards
by deliberate careless showing-off prancing and blowing-off sky-dancing
all the strong silent   stark stalk   everyone awaits the vision-trancing.

§

As if a 'comber' of the sea's surface
reached further than all other waves and,
falling back, gave a seething sound
her wing shuffles overlay all around;
chirping grasshoppers had been starting-up.

Thus at the ill-fated Knarsdale nest
that year, even low-flying has not blest
tactics; man's clumsy interference

Some years' tumbledown with their nettle, bracken
ignorance and prejudice crumble, meddling slacken

§

like other ground-birds, there in the way of being
something hidden behind the range of hill
as Margaret and I came upon them, seeing
suddenly over the crest "the blue hawk" swinging
in and away through all what had been still
and he serving two nests of young, two "ring-tails"
both in view from up here. What if he fails?

Harrowed ground

down off the Blackamoor
on the turning fields
over the magnetite mines
a single bank-vole yields
to three hours' surveillance

oatfields' smoke harvest-sparrows
as suddenly as he appears,
sodden seeds spill where he steers –
his rudders' wake parting.
No attempt at chase of those
A roe's head's up, and starting.

Weary, not expecting further encounter
this evening homing from the harriers
a sparrowhawk on an opposite saunter
almost collides head-on over the barrier
of the Lang Dyke. We stop to banter.

for Alexandra
May 17/18, 2011

§

where the plains stare, and stare back
solitary bird stirs turning their space
bird that the strong sun paints black
as crows, giving way to her greater grace;
who, like them, saw cultivation over common
to reduce her sort and all other such variety
and 'ecology' toward monoculture, mammon...

June, already faded of that year's niggardly seasons
offers mainly worms, wireworms, a few finches
a proud bird of prey's poor picking, thin rubble
we've reduced the surface of Mother Earth to Arable
stiff stems of poor cereals, 'permanent pasture',
converted the top predators into scavengers
– this one's future: doomed, but only a parable...

§

No mower seemed the sharper
– the ring-tail we named "harper",
her hunting no random thing
neatly as the ploughman's skill
 octaves on her passing-strings
scoring the sides of the hill
where the ling-owl is stitching.
Wind in their wings differing
to our ears. And from grasses
subsong. Notes that all *belong* –
their harmonies ring hill still
our humming begins, and passes
to the mind of each, a song
wordless, I hear you sing...

A.J. Munby of York; for a descendant, listening with me (1968)
(Munby: straightest plough lines seem curved on any hill)

22

§

Once over Eskdale, as one
into the rising of the sun
five ringtails soared and, as
over a fjell in Norway
gerfalk family at play.
As surely on some signal
each bird 'stands up on its tail'
climbing fast, as-one display.
Of whale-pod going-away
flukes salute breaking of day.

Eskdalemuir and
North fjords 1955

§

Hear not only near torrents roar,
the rumble of avalanche, of glayciers
but the mountains climb as they soar
ever higher for the elements, lower
the ravens pass the word down, the harriers
by sweeping low, slow give out the score
to all of us below who might hear
in silence. So the larks can take up the song,
the sun helps them. The Great Wind Blower
all knew but never name no matter how long
generations have been coming in from Shore.

Wind's partnership (harrier)

See how he manages economy; flap, soar and stall
his wind; his strength and directing has it skip
along lee of the long dyke at the head-wall
like a tide's rip, the current that lifts lets fall
(shifts grit, silt, sand and all, helps making landscape)
a long-shore-drift moves the hoverer, makes up his mind
pattern of his hunting, herring-bone or front-and-behind,
boustrephodon; whatever the manner his learning to find
bred into him, the low passes either side of this wall
convenient for the required coming-upon surprise
which this slow raptor needs to be able to feed at all –
optimistic the buoyancy? Long wings and so wide
to lift and sail, turn on a sixpence, and use all the whip
of a calmer day – choose bits of it in storm and squall!

Hebrides and Orkney

§

Discerning her rhythms framing last of night
her day ribbons her dales, along with dykelines
black-rimmed, white shadows show relict snowbanks' bright;
not enough light yet to reflect narrowing craglines to dalehead
in flooded ings old haughlands, mirroring instead
her descents to their margins where, as at tide-strand
a few wild duck and Winter-waders still-stand.

Great Northern Floods 1968, 2000

§

Talon scarring assists in the signature
of this individual hen-harrier
carving experience at kill and ploating
carrying dignity as in her floating.

As on the Clevelands we watched a 'short-ear'
catch and be caught by a stoat, we were near –
the one to suffocate, the other to carry a scar
deep into scutellate scales. Over on, far
on Danby, John watches her the next 'vole year'

This ringtail was in Seavy Slack roost with the others
all the next winter, perhaps with her brothers
and sisters – why not a family – only one old bird –
only two used the rock plucking-place and I wondered
how they knew it, seven miles from rendezvous
unless related. A wide moor of similar
outcrops, most giving all-round long view
fairly unhindered at their height, and familiar
surely from their regularly repeated overview…

for James Fisher and Ken Brown

A BlueHawk in January Storm

Tossing the tops of the pines, down below
the wind is in my head; and is it in his?
which bends the moor-grass row by row
(declaring what kind of bad hill-land this is) –
the better for a good brush-out of frass, you know?

Will he adapt his going-round rounds' business
to force 9, and has the wind anything left but to blow
to emptiness; not here has it anywhere else to go
is as alone as anyone else on this black day's hill
yet the harrier has to set out, show willing to kill

perhaps today he needs the wind's assistance
approaching the scattered moorcocks fast down-blast
like a peregrine might flush the odd one at last
after more laborious passes than his, in its teeth
and buffet, not using the 'dead' hollows in the heath

apart from grouse – I missed the other denizen –
apparently asleep still, the highcrags' raven
not tucked under his wing, but laid upon it like lead
he rests his old head on the high roaring watershed
and will pick the grouse bones when this gled has fed…

§

Sweeping The Weel, scene of Tees' high meanders
between least-known fells he spins his wheel –
not for gamblers planning its drowning, far away,
for whom unknown beauty presents no reminders…

(for once, sheep run before him, grumbling;
are they expecting repeat of the bog burst tumbling
down Meldon Fell with no prior warning rumbling
and afterward darkening Tees so they could not drink?)
Sweeping the Weel he is; all grace and spring steel
blue-edged wild-*living* where planners cannot think
but will blunder, – just as my lines are stumbling.

1964, 1968

§

There are, were, four couples south of Cheviot:
one prospecting Gled Scaur flatt by fair Dod Law
not to nest there by Doddington, but in a flaw
of the shining glidder-slacks westward, alight
with the glow off those stones as those dotterels.
White Moss's birds have gone off to Sundaysight
of mixed fortunes, another pair in the forest
favoured a bit of blow-out – but found no rest,
shot-off, like those others far out on the fells…

(1980s)

Lady Moss

for Hugh McDiarmid

see how the hen-harrier harangues
those vole-runs she hangs over yonder
now that the snow, we hope, has gone
and she can see where they dither and wander!

Soon she chooses and swoops, doon-dings
"an gets what's due to her, by jings"
for she'll be master of place, and all Scotland beyond her...

Now just one man, one just man, has gone
independent as that sun that had shone
through that last meeting, haranguing, bringing-on
with it a spirit to emerge from every one
from a life of no compromise anywhere
around its 'hail circumference circumjacked';
jack-of-all-trades as a poet must be, I cracked,
master of one, which is to deliver, to stir
crack, craze the enamelled-over complacency
of the withering ditherers in their ascendancy...

CS to C.M.G (1892-1978)

(1978)

§

Our puzzle of the tossing tassels on the July haughs from our distance
was which way the breeze was there in the shelter of our daleside ridge
silken grasses wave to haytime near, back and forth so that at a glance
they seemed moved in their phalanxes and ranks from the west toward
    the bridge:
but was this action or reaction? We'd see how the harrier would respond:
the wind so slow, close to the seed heads, is not that in the treetops yonder
– lesson of the cricket-field, and of sailing toy boats over the pond…

against the prevailing she floated a constant wind we'd found on the river,
to begin quartering; rising over the levee into it, just one turn to deliver
herself on the start-line. On such a silent morning a pinion creak may
    be heard
above stem-and-husk rustle, any creaks in her rigging may speak to a bird:
just over the tops she glides on the long limb of her quadrilateral
where we've noticed disposition of rabbit and partridge on its 'lands',
and she takes, one swoop on the turn off that approach, and easily suddenly
    stands
on her prey suffocates by talons just as silently and unruffledly
as the wind her partner graces the surface breathings of that sea, as you
    and me
look at each other at last. Already some of our hay is made; she is ploating
hand-in-hand we leave for no place; as unplanned, as light as feathers are
    floating.

1970

§

All the birds in creation
looked on the earth downward
and all learned it but man,
so earth stood man up on two feet
to see across a part of it
and notice such as us occasionally
going about our business.

§

continuous motion, of the gulls as over the sea
to the loss of groundnests' eggs and chicks all spring and summer
(pipits', larks', chats', snipe's, twite's, dunlin's, grouse, two kinds plover
– even, if unguarded at disturbance, curlew, merlin, harrier –
nothing safe from the corvids' patrolling either.

*

here and there the harriers' likewise interminable wander
mingles with the gulls' and gives *them* opportunity for plunder
-the biters bit, by the gamekeeper – unsung!

Education

Tinselling lichen and fern-fronds springing silver and gold
the pullets through bracken and borran snicket and alley
ungainly, stiffly stumbling numb as I am in the cold
noises dumbed under rumbling of water through their gully
sully their straggly down and struggling unruly young shafts
wing-tripped and tail-turned plodging sivs in wet sphagnum moss
rust and silver-stemmed *Polytrichium*, thin crusts of fungus...

Yet they are finding, its early for spiders 'eggs' in holes;
pupae, and resting-stages of insects, beetles and bugs,
crustacea... their parents are bringing-in water-voles
as well as meadow-voles and off the bogs the early frogs
and show the skinning for some, for most the swallowing whole
and once, how to keep an eel still enough to kill, by feel
underfoot by pads and talons, combining cushion and steel.

Then the show of vole-runs thrown-up by 'quartering', flight
and squinting off dyke and boulder for the angle of light
and shadow, or which mowdie-heap gives motion from below
perhaps by watching the kestrels' hovering, or the crow.
Growing-up on top of their midden of bones may be quite
an anatomy lesson once they've greedily stripped them right
learned the grips and the cuts as a master butcher might!

Foddering on the Fell   (Forster's, 1960)

Oh, she'll mebbe bide yonder, you know
whee old cussenberry stands in snow
– where an eagle hunted that winter and I
divided term time with where the falcons fly*

*

under the cirrus' lace, these graces in space
but underwings showed twice a hunger-trace
when I watched near enough from behind my dyke
the assembly at roost, not again there to see the like

*

Black forest-blocks, Corbies, blackgame
black gallowas, black dykebacks and black clouds
shading greys by grades, of drifts, of his wings
lightening to pearl under the occasional light-swirling
when the mind shifts as his patterns shape-shift
to blue-and-white quite bright for a very short shrift
as the sky becomes mirk from overcast, purple with snow
blue-hawk hues from Cambridge blue to slate or stone
(Stone-slate, welsh slate, Coniston slate, basalt, bone)
when rooks look brown, stoggies white from grey
as surely evolving together for the eyes in the skies.

* *gyrfalcon studies Westmorland that winter*

§

wing through, not over, learn on her terms
her world we would usurp carelessly
not to ask her finding weigh ahead
along her esker under her dead
once-glacier, now brushed ceaselessly
as she seeks summer rains' worms, blood-worms;
lengthening and strengthening in the sun the way she's come
tilting horizons dizzying once-easy footsureness
out of the blue of the grey she lifts leaning light lemming
adjusts her grip lest wet fur slips, stops combing the stemming
tussocks fresh of the spring green promise of prey regardless –
on her wind and the tundra's breeze everything else is dumb

Norway 1955

§

Dead-bracken den we sciving bairns warm
– this hill-farm's outbye, in lambing-storm
for the harrier's nest, that last year
four eggs forever, for that so rare…

Another, that season's, on a military range
also only four – were all these first-breeding birds?
This was not a vole-scarce year, so strange
two other nests have five: one three – as sherds…

North of England, 1955

§

On an almost-daily route through the High Pennines on foot towards the nearest harrier roost there is a place I call the 'staked plains' – after the 'llanos estocados', Staked Plains, in the half desert by the Texas Panhandle. Here, a number of poles and stakes, not obvious to the passerby on the nearest right-of-way, stick up out of the heather and bent tussocks. Today, sunny all day at last here, I watched a harrier make for the roost in the usual desultory fashion; perhaps half-heartedly hunting, or merely idling. A huge hen bird, bigger than a buzzard apparently in the golden light toward sunset, great dihedrals low over the heather like the cruck of a tree silhouetted, the angle that of the sharpest profile of Scarth Nick. She settled, with a flourish up-and-fold of the long wings, facing the sun on one of the taller posts. Bathed in the light, rudding over the next twenty minutes, she sat utterly ignoring me, or unaware as she faced away. And I tried a photograph but of course it was into the sun... After those 20 minutes another smaller immature bird arrived, 'greeted' her with wing-stretches in the air beside her and settled on a post nearby, having had her almost off her perch with surprise. Both seemed to sleep, one hunched, the other upright; her face literally sheepish in its broadness. Eventually, and still short of the dark, the third member – 3 are all that are 'left' of the number which used to roost together – turned up out of the sun and also neck-buffeted each of the other two, as if a greeting of that sort was required. Perhaps it is... Anyway, 3 is the 'roost' there – I wonder whether the others are temporarily absent, detained (trapped, shot, migrated elsewhere?) or now 'courting'.

§

– why so long on the same fencepost
but a perch where she watches the dale most
turning only a little but in and out of the sun
her dull shroud shifting a little, as if for fun
showing her long legs a little in the wind
deceives us by nonchalance; her eyes have spinned
with her head, owl-like, the bluff of her ruff
pulled as if only by wind, taking her scruff
is on us. Upon her stilts now, she struts her stuff
a step or two onto the wind, but a crow closes
from behind, retreats, complacent, now she dozes.

§

Full sun on pasture daisies gives the same sheen
of silver as on the Bluehawk

this 'santerin' cloud on its westerly is the westerly
there is no other evidence of wind that I feel or can see;
the grasses laid over stationary, yet the harrier can fly
float under it with the kestrel and I wait and wonder why
– after many watchings in wind I find this scene quite often;
birds watching the clear-cut edge work where the ground softens
to shadow of the stately cloud encroaching from brightness
– perhaps a prey is confused at the edge of dark and lightness
– so often I've seen the meadow vole in sun but yet in cover, still, basking
– when it moves suddenly its taking seems there 'for the asking'…

On Urra Moor, Lilla, or wherever I couldn't get higher
I'd lie on my back and ask hawks and larks of entire sky:
for those days gone by I long as if these days didn't try…
ever since, stronger and stronger the developed desire.

§

on a gust
swirl of clouds and mist
we saw the thing fall
right in front of us
so we had to stop
to pick it up and look at it
– part of the limb of a lamb…

*

on a curse of the wind
it has fallen to us
or by calculation.
Bird (or scavenger?) had partly skinned
(by marks of the culmen)

*

Bird I had watched days
at the common, surely.

*

On a whim of communication?
mischief or a mislay?
we wish we could say…

for E.M. Makepeace, the Tyne Gap, 1986

3 Ringtail Poems, with old Tommy

1.
In a moment of being, "is" is how he put it –
up Trollas Gill the evening-glow; 80-odd-year old.
His words for this hill didn't shift the ringtail off it
as mine for the ringtail did in greeting, off her post
before we realised we'd put her up from her kill
(still warm, so we took that grouse with us, exposed to the core)
The farmer here, his neighbour once, stole Tommy's sheep off here before…

2.
in objectivism; the poem is, as, an object (ZUK.)
– and it needs dealing with, preparing, as such
– as much an object, and as above; as, look
the best of them should take flight in us
as the bird must, to be a bird. For some,
for others, this is the weakness of our view
– see it sits its post just as an owl might do…
we had prepared the bird already in the mind-
like the poem a concept, and that's how we find
"All objects are either extant or not…
what's for 'spotting' is not 'put on the spot'"

1999, North Pennines

3.
'half-owl flies when the day-hawks are blind
half-'ling-owl', spanning beyond that kind
after first movement over the bog on the fell
greys merge with browns, tones merge pell mell
with wing action so low that the winds' waves
of the heather and grasses echo, are her slaves
like the wagon wheels pour the wath's wash
more than part it, part of its churn and slosh
arbitrary as any unexplained bit of freshet

A Ring-Tail's Insistence

She is up here, as I am, in her way, for fun
if only in such light to see for long distances
offering week-long weakening long slant from the sun
horizon familiar soon for all cloud-bellied distances
passages she titled, introduced in proportion
– believing withering lights mirage = existences
exuberance of her sailing and coming winter caution

Colsterdale, Winter '73/'74

§

In grip of winter bitter winds will not bother to stir
– at times it is so cold the sun himself makes little blaze
to warm himself, where the sky is clear for nights and days
and is hardly strong enough to cast a low long shadow;
when the Blue Hawk is thus one with the blue and white of snow
and so goes unseen and low below billows and curricks
and the cairns up here standing for his and our way-marks,
sometimes like prayer pennants with wind blowing summit-plumes
of new snow. And coming on at height before gloaming looms;
once and once only in many years there for me a gyr
stands handsome and recent from who knows where to who knows where

Remembering Spring Hill Fog

(With David Pearson, Cross Fell, 1954)

a dotterel is false-security up here
personified, but far from petrified of fear
at me, my legs and scuffed boots so near
his or her delicacy squat in the pelseneer
rough upended boulders, raw since the glacier
frost-shattered at different angles of rake
jumbled graveslabs after an earthquake
a softness is its own beauty. 'Cock-Laik'
down below, where the blackcocks ratch and rake
once showed us a trip of nine, for their sake
we made a wide berth on a compass-steer
and it was then the harrier found us, awake
suddenly at his appearance; unearthly drear
fell-clouds in in his lichened grey, gleam on a wet fence-stake.

§

Distant from the hayfields its Yellow Rattle
transhumant as any pastoral nomad
'blue-hawk' on the wind combs through rushes' tresses
a 'Simmer Wetter' like that in Wensleydale
where my neighbour summered his black hill cattle
robbing Robber-flies; mince-pies on his scale
under sky empty of cloud, a land of wings
reflecting its silvernesses, greennesses,
bluenesses, greynesses, pulsing shimmerings
oasis mirages second-nature for harriers
seasonally such as found the Aral Sea

(1988) Greenlee Lough, Northumberland

§

August; autumn setting-in with 'some weather east-coast',
hairst hardly in, but 'Buck' relieves dust in the throat…
steep dale sides spread their raglan sleeves at haytime
slashed darkly, seamed-down, with sikesides' sivs which chime
linings of avens and meadowsweet, yarrow
brightening, geraniums' deepening glow.
Blue-hawk, arriving with the gull patrols, floats
where 'Intak Jack' last tried to grow fother oats
when both were talked about tolerantly at Show
back o't' 'Buck', though few knew either of them;
each up so early, even for those men then
and living apparently alone, even
for those days' ways biding to stay remote.
The one, gone to 'stones', the other to a 'gurt stoat'.

§

Doubt everything, and equally;
that these green bracken-shoots will mature
to hide the nest quite sufficiently
when leggy young will rise to stand sure.

For now, the eggs are sung-over by a pipit
so no nest-scavenger yet has a hint of it:
a little mist of its own rises
off midden and platform, brooder absent
perhaps to drink, but miles off she flies
while nearby the bog and sikes' scent
violet and acid, acrid in heat-wobble
yet she steers back, carreers cobbily
drops by the gleg-hole, ignoring my bottle.

1993

To Roost

"moor-buzzard" (name of harrier often for some)
'before the sun has arrived' he is already come,
settles on a bare capstone along yon yowe-shelter
wind has kept clear of 'lambing-storms' snowy welter,
whereas the old snow's fair scalloping the lingy fell,
whiles, along a little, I'm finding a place to ligg
where I can watch him, and scan the line of this long rigg.
cold the night to come and cold the hill, but I tingle
warm with the watching as in the cosiest ingle!

(yowe: ewe, lingy: heathery, ligg: lie, rigg: ridge)
1960, Cleveland

§

"Pullt" children with catapults –
pocket-money from the ironmongers
at the Corner of Stokesley High Street
(better ones for the growing hunger –
from George Hardwick, Stubbs or Jack Hatfield

after we'd made our own; forked
twigs of ash, tormented all, and hawked
Sphagnum moss off the bogs to florists'
and a new craze for hanging baskets...

Thus armed, early trip to the Catrails
for grouse and partridge by 'Excelsior'
breaking the skin of the earth, these swales
wilder than home's Blackamore
(wider moors, but lower, of lesser scale)
– and there a first, unhurrying harrier
came over us as if we were not there
after the same game; it all seemed unreal,
but such grace began to make us *feel*:

Ringtail Harrier

Coming-on over on the wave of her energy
shower-clouds progressively prospecting and quartering
yet getting no nearer and half-staring ignorance
curtains curtail each range of each other, and then condense
in rain detaining a shrunken sunset, bringing gloam
off the Cross Fell range of summits, and still she will roam
a part of, apart from, weather and heather, the synergy.

Over the Bewcastle Fells the rough sandstone
dips to the north or northwest; its crags
facing south or west with the lovely linns
(no 'fosses' here) – their waterfalls and rapids.
From the Cussenberry Craigs at altitude
of distorted strata-form consistent attitude
present hollows, basins, tabletops "for her comfort"

for Reginald Bell

§

oxidised stone-stripes run red downscree
badge of scrambling-honour to this child, me
– ochred fingers and knees, the seeing dale
ought to overlook the idiot at his scale
(before he took up scree-running one day –
fresh scars festooning the screes his way…)

but soon on his knees again on another cause
– lizards drag themselves out along the hawse
sluggish in late winter, early spring hazard
the harrier, more alert then than their regard…

Harrier in mem. Alan Ridley

Cock harrier, light then dark, turned-over the hollows
using the cloud-shadows sculpting along, across, the hill
testing us in and out over and under where we can't follow
for surely if we could we'd be up with the blue-hawk still!

His mate, perhaps, or another ringtail hurrying time, occasion
across our bows who know only loose 'nows' in succession
has a long purpose we learn to descry in time, to kill
at last the black-cock marked-down a mile away of will

And such we'd not deny them; we've shot cocks out of the wood
shaking scores of berries out with the scatter-drops of blood.
But these birds after days of picking at roadkill "Kinnen*
and yance hung about us when we were at skinnen"…!

(2009)
* Kinnen: rabbits

A Portal for a Mortal

Spiky amongst the landslip pinnacles, ferns
and foxgloves' corpses: the spires of folded birds
birds tall old gaunt and still but for the detail
of downy contour-feathers showing a scale
of origin of outline, gathering gloom

to come off the fell on foot the evening
with the goad riding irresistible urge
surf-ride of windy heather a leavening
 of the load lifting, enlivening wave surge
where out demanding lives yet leave them room

the sisters mustered-in from their hunting grounds
off to sleep statuesque, separate, standing
sculptures deft drapery, primaries wrapped round
a master's touch, the grotesque in his handling
to incubula around cathedral tomb

surf-ride back of joy at lack of disturbance
sheep hardly shifted throughout this yowe-trummle
no flight-lines deflected by my surveillance
but once out of range leaping tufts I tumble
bruise up an out-of-season ling-bloom…!

§

What we observe is not nature itself but nature exposed to
our method of questioning (Heisenberg)

    [Overheard on the 'bus to Hexham:
    "A *bloody* big gull, with a face like an owl
at the Market Cross came right down to the ground"
out of the blue, a lot of hill-fog beyond
yes, this was broad day otherwise, in Alston
and "scuffed along up to the Top of the Town"
inches above the empty cobbles and setts
(for it was six o'clock in the morning, yet)

And wasn't that the morning, John Alderson,
postman getting ready, had one 'bout the roofs
of The Firs' estate, and sees well from his house
beside the cemetery like some silver ghost
(John, well taught by his father about naming's proofs)
observer I'd learned to trust then more than most,
and tell me carefully lighting-up his round.

There are those who have, over lifetimes,
a few anecdotes of 'Blue' and of 'Marsh' 'Hawks',
'Moor Buzzards', called 'gleds' at other times
and because such names are, no more than squawks,
accepted as "accurate" of species
dismissed, not recognizing all this richesse
has been a constant demon of some "science":
the story is as in the bone as poetry is
does not need to come out; or, if it does,
the cauldron might dissolve away or disguise
the meat no matter how hard the hunter tries.

Padding Words Stalk

As the record droned on, I realised
that the voice was of e.e. cummings
though there were imagined capitals
each word allowed to do its own work
distinct in scatter of little birds
needing no punctuation, predicating diction
nuclear and patterned patter, to matter.
Not needing breathing space around it but using it well
enough for me to set down figurine, leviathan
of caravans coming, camels padding soft over Indiana dunes
to that pouring of grit, or those hoppers' continual for the furnace
at Gary; that harrier hanging on wind for Harry
laughing in our faces the spaces between feathered fingers.
Everyone else realizes that the record is still running-on.

(Indiana, 1973)

§

'ALBEDO' – reflected light off ice and snow
and we'll stretch it to white sand beaches' glow
these strandflats and machair, Longisland Hebrides
where graceful gleds glide long, land breeze and seabreeze
and themselves glow with the silver of sea and land
as glaucous as sea-holly, glaucous and grey and
white, blue-grey white the cock-birds "blue-hawks"
the stately fulmars mock. But harriers hunting auks?
No, he is plucking an oiled guillemot for its fat
– undignified, perhaps; but we hawk-watchers leave it at that.
None of us claimed the harriers were *falcons*
except Linnaeus, and he'd not the opportunities given to us
with his eyes to the ground for plants and such fuzz
but he must have known the albedo and its welcome!

§

Land gone under flood.
She brings back the land
with the green Prothonatary
I had failed to see
but, used to haugh-land
going under, no wonder
I saw the dull brown harrier
a mile away over her river

Long brown wings quiver
to no terraces' pasture
she sparred with the spectre –
somehow a dragonfly –
(this is April, not July,
Wisconsin, not North Yorkshire.

1973, In mem. Lorinne Niedecker

§

Until late I follow her regular round some days
and notice unusual apparent absence, shortage
of some species amongst her personal list of prey
preferred; remembering how Feynman said of a bird
that to have named it, whether it's' sighted or heard,
is not even to begin to know it – tell *that* to "birders"!

But if you can't name it right, you can't even begin
to study it, enlighten with, say, what family it is in...
There's 'nature lore' in these transhumance herders,
and this otherwise-disciplined describer of nature –
harrier's ability to empty her route is kin
to other hunters', suggesting a thin classification
and identity beyond histology. Not one feature,
or even many in anatomy, links true structure.

Central Asia 1987

§

Her fear transmits to me, as mine to her,
– for I fear for her and her young behind
long legs – she's risen to her full height to scare
'ground-vermin' – tussocks' nest to us so hard to find
in long-grass prairie and marsh-edge sedge. To share
a first emotion of the hunter's, of the hunted's mind.

Her young rear up, and face me fiercely
when I trespass the critical distance, see
like marmots (their parents' prey) and silently –
then hissing and spitting, fire flaring wildly
thrust even at my shadow, then my shoes, daringly
as if these boots killed their kind, and unsparingly

§

Reed between the lines of our flooding-survey
something harriers and the other birds would purvey
in glimpses and long study there day day after day

rudded to blood at sunrise and sunset
suddenly their birds seemed in summer plumage

shining flooded ings' marvel of these levels
Marvell* would have known, over east on The Hull's

thousands of waders and wildfowl, in gathered populations
drawn to the water-meadows, draw the peregrines
the hawks, the harriers, and those of us also, smitten –
still, forty years on, as truly hard-bitten!

*For John and Jeff, Margaret and Susan
the Yorkshire Derwents, 1968-2009*

(*the poet Andrew Marvell)

§

I see her standing stark against the snow
and seeming swollen, a post with enlarged shadow
over the swallow-hole, full sun, an hour or so
steady as a heron, made of the same stuff
a-glow about the nape as a merlin, her ruff
brushed-up, excited, gives her that sort of look
as a long-eared owl on alert. Wonder-struck
I see her eyes even close, as I slowly close-up
stop at the dyke, but its sike's snipe rose-up
and switch backed away – she'd been probing below
through snow and catice. Didn't the harriers do?
No, she has opened only one dark eye to show
in defiance, or careless, of what she must know
hearing me closer that I now wanted to go.
She has killed and eaten, was falling asleep
my surprise and privilege. I left her to rest.
Hours later and late to her roost, I gave best,
came home with a will, where I sometimes creep…

[Water voles' tails discovered,
Tynehead January 8th, 2008]

(Upper Teesdale)

An hour to get up over the sodden
ravine but glad of the way weather given
Thor or Odin – driven these seven
the *Snout*, or Snot, *Cataracts*
foaming over whinstone tracts
white on black 'greenstone' basalts
mighty (as) Alaskan, Icelandic
Kanchatkan torrent-riven faults
giving the lie to parallax
spray for a mile on this terrific
storm hail and black rain blasts
warm "silingdoon" stair-rods downdale
forgotten; the scramble against
force, worse than up at Sourmilk
Gill, sheltered by its father-hill
But there across the steamy rim
of the Cauldron's edge in its clouds
at the uppermost ledge, the proud
elegant slow passage, long sliver
wings' blues message, harrier
rides master of all turbulence
finds my calm centre commonsense
sadness at his future prospects
of finding a mate on grouse moor
these days, for some of the poor
keepers and beaters and shepherds
would take the 'reward' for these birds...

*(memories, and notes, 1949-1956
and revised 2000)*

§

a bird made for the wind-spinning world of their
own as albatross and shearwater are
or catabatic's ten-knot 'regular',
the tundra's, the steppes; the prairie's,
the fells', high plateaux', machair's
dune-systems' and strands' beside the seas
the great rivers' and the weather-fronts' airs

no other than harriers have such wrists
flexing those primaries the way they twist
and churn air – perhaps hence 'harrower'
over a dry field's dust, torque vortex

for weight and wind-weight to resist
mass hangs from those wing-tips
broad for the uplift and the flex…

Black Band

Coming off Black Band (too much unburnt hydocarbons – 4WD!!) I was aware of something else behind me. I didn't turn at first, thinking it might pass me (in the air, or a hare near to the side). After a moment or two I realised it wasn't going to but was even closer and staying there, behind. So I half-turned, and a ringtail about 10 yards directly behind rose easily on one wingflap over my head and away at an angle of 45° without haste. Why had she 'hung' behind me? Not 'quartering', this old girl (a weary 'red' face, leg scarred in the left tarsus – mebbe indeed from a ring –) smoothly lost height behind the straggly but thriving wood wedge from Fiona's and sailed directly over the Tynehead road and kept the pines the other side between us as she *did* start to quarter the pastures beside Pasture House and toward the 'ring-ousel' bank. This took about 17 minutes – she lifted into the air at the end of her quartering there and shot the Ashgill bridge and was lost to sight toward, and nearly at, Priorsdale. This bird has hunted about here previous dawns – from the nearby roost where there are 5 or 3 others most nights (half-moon or less) but I haven't seen her catch anything yet.

24th February 2007

§

When summer air "won't bear mair than a prayer"
for a breeze
when the shy spirit moves at last, and at least
expect stilling
of a breathing day and onto a level that lifts
grasses' stems, ferns, bog-cotton to their full height
expands displays toward seeds for their dispersion
open to eye skies ovaries
stumbles the dumble-dor and the bumble-bee

then the spirit that fills lungs as it opens nostrils
present thyme and first violet, brings on in
swifts where the nightjar dares not
shadowless and immaterial with the bog-owl
rises the harrier our sense of the love of land
a mood more than a bird between us, moment
that will not hurry her, patterned as heath-moth;
moths she collects as she sees, trails their powder
cracks pleasure of dor-beetles and bumble-bees

§

traipses the bounds of the forest blocks
and into them where they show their rock
outcrops and rides, a few wing spans wide
and the bird can navigate a little inside:
these woods were harrier nurseries years ago
roe put their heads aslant and gesture slow
untroubled by her silent pass and sudden shadow

§

No 'visitations of locusts' yet
but the desert has its swarms;
some cloudburst storms
scores of voles   break the seams
bog bursts of rodent their hunters get
grasshoppers, craneflies, the gleams
of groundbeetles and dungbeetles shine
amongst jewels of raindrops shaking free
hanging on breaths of wind; how fine,
how few there are come here to see!…

§

As if out of our bivouac, stiff with no skills,
all wings and legs and tail and ruff roughed
buffeted as tussocks in a gale, this weather
rumbling like a gill-brack high in the hills
scruffy enough to appear emaciated
as a wet heron or one skinned-out to stuff
she gives the horizon's sky her extra blether

stalling at the grasp of last-gasp starling
she comes a tumble-stumble down the stair
starling's bill struck in her undercarriage
until shaken free and she mounts again
(we find the starling dying in its warm stain
on the Solway head marshes; nothing there
to tell whether the harrier would manage…

advance of sky across clear day, blue-hawk glare
sun dances in by, loss of the eye's defence
as looking into its orb, for the distance
doesn't matter – all illusions wobble
deceive as if the harrier carried a hobble
in her cumber of air her lumber of wing
no thermal on apparent lethargy of air.

§

Within fine snow now blowing hard
wind pulling downdraught drawing into this little gill
as the weather turns around under the scarp
grouse out of hanging-about snow-haze still
a moment as it opened fanwise, reverse-torrent
up the gill-head, lifting flecks off dry trees below –
sifting as thin soot, silt from its current.

A lifting scissoring clipping top snowed rifts
winnowing, wingsound surges beyond bank-full,
blue hawk materialises; shape-shifted herring gull!
Best of that sharp snowlaid dais bright gifts
(not forgetting your good picnic under the trees).
Grouse-packs shift after him, with the snow drifts.
He's gone, and his moment lost, high above the Tees;
neither grouse nor gled has seen us, we reckon,
but you haven't seen either – one passing apparition:
Clearing wind has made his mind up as to direction,
the moment gained and lost us in a few seconds.

for Mary

§

She larks along, dotting the line of swallow-holes
pock-marked outcrop, shell-holes without shrapnel
dips out of sight a few seconds in each one, rolls
yaws to her right to the next and next wet hollow
sweeps a little of its lip clear of its shawl of snow
the next squall will renew. Under that snow yellow
grass feeds voles, their saffron stains she will know
Jim says she's a spread-like a Solway haaf-net
I knew the hole she tarries at only for its Burnet
last backend. Now I know it for her killing a water vole
where even ling owls and kestrels had shown little interest.

55

One of the hunted

Hours counting the peewit territories
from this fell side above, courting curlews
and a few of the goldies* already sitting;
their plaints anxiety embody –
I take up station where the ravens choose
and watch kestrels at another newcomer
daren't, don't, press home attack to point of hitting…

                    *

In the space between two bleats of the wind swings
that other master of wavelength falls
(even more than the regular gulls are) –
a blue-hawk, using the wind's pulsings,
against him and tangential,
to 'come by' the flock of fieldfares grounded now
a hatch of craneflies. Joe's collie dogs are far.

                    *

I'm hidden still in the pleats of this limestone
and will use its dolines on my approach
but whose purpose is served? they're up and away!
– yet one flies into his grasp and is gone.
Thus positives on error encroach…
That hunter dips over me as in salute,
nothing gives me more careless thought this day

March 30, 2012
* 'goldies' - Golden Plover

Talk with a man who had known Black Elk

"Some wore your" (birds of prey) "on their heads
to go to war" – some naked otherwise
and all these amongst the bravest men
and because here all these rivers rise
our brothers on earth-mother…

*

"Like us, our fore fathers, these hawks
chose the shelterless plains, left the woods"
I put it to him, The People came the hawks followed
like the dogs, to places like Sika Hollow
"No, the Sisseton have not all the Teton blood…"

*

We were on the former Milk River pastures
the bison coming back to northern Montana
though the great ranges are gone. Reverse Migration
is in the heart and mind. Then we went to find
the hawks he thought were   imagination

*

As we *had* imagined it, from Manderson
and Pierre, patches of true Prairie persisted
here and there, and the hawk still visited them
and the farms and townships, "insisting
on adaptation, the only hope for anyone."

§

Cock red-grouse red cockades progress a Hare path
ahead of the harrier's heather-tops pass –
and he makes no deviation, and no dash –
and all their heads go down again in a flash
to darkness, silence, no challenging "go back".
Hackles depressed in fear or an emotional wreck
heartbeats of the hunted are up with death for the slack.

§

Harriers come with the swiddening's* reek-swirls
curl and tower in clear air in spring's unfurls
and me building pulse on the moor as on the prairie
and something of their swinging flight is in a harmony
as are the lapwings' and curlews' display – flights
larks and pipits yo-yoing evening and even nights.
They don't know, or don't sense, the hunter will be back;
and here he is, minutes later, and on a different tack
into the wind, not so different a dihedral as curlew's at first sight
to stop in mid-bar the gawdie's pipe, the curlew's skirls,
chases the lark lightly up, like the merlin's mounting – alongside
and the lark is still singing as he is gripped (my ears still ringing);
as if the volume would put the harrier off, the outstretched talon
both birds wild-fluttering, the smoke not choking but stinging…

* 'swidden' – *heather burning rotation for grouse management*
'reek' – *smoke*

58

§

one of the ripple hollows ribbing the hill
gargoyle over glog-oil keeping very still

if I walk too fast when he's up, up to it,
try to get too close; I'll trip…
it's like any other tryst

time after time waits on me
not as the falconer's bird, aloft or on the wrist

let no other intrusion on this hollow ground
they've chosen in this gill as hallowed, found
for the winter shelter amongst places all around
'as suitable'

does the hawk *need* the presence of a 'person'?

  not haunting the hills
but showing the man, the man alone at first

calls of the wading-bird own the fell
tell of me and the harriers just as well

("glog-oil" – hole in peaty ground)

for Margaret Hartley
2001, 2012

§

Their colour becomes their shape, in the fell's hues
their contours define them as their own surely do
 changing with them and clouds and light, the blues
grey and the greens lighten and darken and merge
red dead cottongrass swards to a sable serge
with the heather mixture as dead. But the urge
is from sun and shadows chasing, life to emerge –
silvered beetles; rusting butterflies and moths fly
as soon as the sun and a million brilliant flies
fill for the pipits and larks lower parts of the skies

she has not swallowed craneflies since November
(she presents the undigested evidence and I remember
yet knows where they'll not be bigger until September)...
this ringtail harrier, though she will not breed
stays on these fells (scores of square miles, she'll need)
and there are very few of us to take even any heed
let alone persecute her these days of a *reduced* greed.
She rattles the rushes ahead of us like hail does
and we welcome her presence but without much fuss
lest the 'twitchers' hear – not much in common with us!

Harriers Digesting Rodents at Roost

Here – last winter they used the edge of the young trees –
two ringtails cough up a long casting from each
an hour apart, but scarce any other motion
until a stretching long wing seems to just over-reach
massively and catches the wind capsizing commotion
shifting the other haggards, clumsy uneasy witches
shuffle from this one, this one I name 'Meg Merrilees'…

leaning lichened gravestones seen sideways
marker-posts at the old shaft
or where a steeper swalley scars the surface
need reckoning in the stalker's craft
deepen silence because what can not be seen
(and 'experts' overlooked water-voles here
whether 'dry', or their walls 'too sheer')

'water-voles' misnamed in these uplands
live in bogs, peat hags, clints and grikes,
some rank bracken, rush clumps and siv stands
all sorts of cover by slightest sikes;
mustelids and harriers and gulls know well
the ways of *three* voles on the high fell
– three shrews too; rats, woodmice, more 'small deer'…

§

Two hen-harriers in one day, hunting adjacent stints of the Stainmore-Swaledale fells and gills, details of dales and swales, the boggy and grassy rises and flatts, the lambs and curlews and peewits, if not the heafed sheep and hares and pipits, rabbits and larks. A grouse panic only when the ringtail turned to repeat a patrol high over them. Where men named their places simply, as if there were not other 'kelds' and thwaites beyond theirs or these the harriers marked the farms – in those days of the 'fifties and 'sixties still small 'mixed' farms with shorthorns and 'swardills' – for poultry and volesward, potential good hunting grounds.

Over the carved fells her curves linked a pattern early May morning set and confirmed; the 'ringtail' female harrier a buzzard-like figure where buzzards were then as scarce as harriers and as generally 'discouraged'. My friend Ernie's farm welcomed either for their work against rabbits – competitors with his sheep for his good grass, and valued the merlins on his fell, which tried every year to rear young in one or other, sometimes two when the first clutch was taken by boys or 'vermin', heathery braes with good aspect over part of the dale. My sister and I knew only one other farmer, at the dalehead, who appreciated birds of prey…

Never tiring of watching any of these more or less predictable presences, once we had found them, and enjoying especially the hide-and-seek in cloud ('hill fog') and rain, we learnt to follow the clues from the calls of the wading birds nesting on the same ground. The curlew seemed then to have a different warning, to chicks and neighbours, when a harrier was about to when a fox was, a stoat, or a man.

Just even more rarely than 'either' harrier (and we were never sure these bred there, but once…), the spring usually brought a peregrine falcon or two, and rarely a pair bred in Swaledale's remoter reaches or not far away. Once a 'keeper pointed out an even more magnificent visitor, the peregrine's bigger relative a gyrfalcon, which I had already encountered in Norway and Iceland and was to become 'obsessed' by… But we went years with hardly a buzzard in the sky, then; and indeed saw more, in one particular winter and early spring (springs are late in Swaledale, as elsewhere in the North Pennines!) of that magnificent occasional winter hunter the Rough-legged Buzzard – understandably mistaken in the dale then as no less than a Golden Eagle!

Absent from these scenes, apparently, some years, the yet-present taken-for-granted, Kestrels and Sparrowhawks!

A 'blue-hawk' came over the pines that evening; short strokes, with the wind behind him that cold damp ENE wind of those past several days but not with rain, sleet or hail *for once*... April 'lambing showers', lambing storms and squalls. A squall this quite dramatic bird, and he passed us with uncommon speed and was out of sight downhill, never mind what I've just written about the sort of weather and visibility there was, in moments. We went down after him but never saw him again, looking this way and that, and, baffled, gave him best. That season we saw no other, but a few men out on the fell every day did see and did not report what they'd seen, as, often, in the instinct of avoiding 'fuss and bother'.

§

big brown gled, grey-blue gled, well met, well matched, their young hatched
alight (right word, illuminating their North Waste patch)
her deep yellow web-hatchings; his pied expanse of wings
reflex-uplift-on-arrival, flashing broad silver-linings
tread so lightly amongst their eyasses bringing
the one a mole caught beside the Lyne floods; the other
a stoat in a gin she'd first had to cover and smother
and then cut free, leaving a leg behind (keeper to curse 'fox'.)
To feed five young? But they see every pipit rise…
an hour later these two brought in a brace of moorcocks
(which surely they can't outfly, must have taken by surprise)
…gleds are of two such contrasting, such unlikely, kinds
"we must now, mek oot – their Maker must have been of two minds!"
– at Fred's house near Hethersgill the old shepherd stills
the room (both senses of 'still') with the crack of the time
(we added stock-dove, partridge, young rabbits to these kills…)
Tommy Elliott doesn't believe the tale until
it's put into "altogether shape, and better rhyme"!

Bewcastle Wastes,
1976 and 2008

§

She works the pastures and meadows like a shepherd
looking for dropped lambs, and nothing then can be heard…

Redletter day; a skylark singing from a post
for all the birds of prey lifted my spirits most
force seven to nine the bright high sky before squalls
expected presently   after the raven-calls
she makes passes between, as the winds' grasses sweep,
raising a few filaments of hair nearest sheep
close passes. Close the 'keeper showed me just *how* close!

Ferns, brackens, beckon, nod their heads to the good ground
over heady grasses, under the dipping harrier;
tall fern flapping similarly, consonantly.
Neither give warning to the player of this facility
his faculty. For even the shower not arbitrary
we watched coming on, harrier's ruff cocked as constantly,
tail flailing with male-fern, trailing the beat, around.

for Close the 'keeper and Graham the shepherd
ad hoc *music in the pub, shepherds' neets*

§

at her most owl-like *(Speotyto)*
she leads her pullets – see them go!
walking, stalking, on the high meadow
(Big Horn Rockies, Absaroke plateau)

two prisms: she shows two faces
to miss nothing, vision peripheral
the under-rated hunter graces
tread as soft as tiger, marshy places
head swinging steady, purposeful
tail-jib in the wind, progress spinned
summer seed-heads, legs at full measure
tarsus-deep in the glories of the pasture
untrodden since the bison. Behind,
her brood grinned, at combat-interval

Winter, south Siberia, another two prisms;
a Kolinsky's, of similar effectiveness
the other side of a snowbank to her
and as part of it; both after rodents
under but not invisible; their scents
and signs obvious, you don't need to 'know' them
don't need insight for love to fit the glove…

§

no matter how 'bleak' to you and I
any plain brightens under his eye
— part of his advantage over us! —
see his wingspan silver this May's fuzz;
green haze of birches busting bud so
they lose their outlines there far below
green baize of bog lands here above:
he chooses to line by the sheer love
his attention is, mate on the ground
— there's no such fellow for miles around! —
now he gyres up and higher still
soundless spirals the whole Fells' air fill

*

the timing of these wingbeats says he is prospecting
and chiming of his arrival before his buzzard rival
for the voles are feeding where we have been expecting
and their holes are behind their forays a way to find
in this grey before day. He's up 'on stilts' to his full height
walking where he's seen their runs, stalking up the moon-light
lest shadows betray him, only yards short of his quarry

'Blue Hawk' places

Part of the fragrance of the map in his mind and mine
thyme and violets, grasses, sphagnum, fern, heather, share
distinctive at all times, as Cheviot from this Pennine
where he's only on certain grounds, and not because he's 'rare'.

*

he knows the patch of fellside that Elliott Ridley sold
better even than my merlin does – but not that raven;
who, like the harrier, has been lucky to grow old —
remembers every fold in the hill, every cold spring
the rabbits' and hare's lawns, field voles' and water voles' even
and where each, eight, species of juicy ground beetle prefer,
where lizards bask early, rare spots earth's laid herself bare;
the season's eggs and nestlings under his censer's swing.

*

I don't live in their world and won't; already
how often I've found them, fooled by 'Sat Nav',
many road miles from where they wanted to be...
whereas this bird, 'territory' undefined but to have
within it all and more of the open fells I can see;
knows the ground – better than I do – but like me...

§

learning from him to use the contours
to hide myself, down on an elbow
crouching, crouch-climbing-scrambling lures
alarms, tell-tale shadow on the snow...

§

piping with, and like, the gawdies over there,
yet less mournfully; at times almost a blare
for this is 'territorial-light' proclaiming
and more than one mate he might soon be claiming;
I've seen three 'ringtails' on this fell in three miles
and he hovers over each of these earthworks
their heather and rushes proud of bevelled earth

vortices and long swoops live on the air
after manoeuvres are finished, and I still stare
driving me from becoming a gamekeeper
blaming any and all 'hookbills' ever steeper
into oblivion. But we – first mercy for the merlin –
managed a little for the harrier, hiding a few
and they'd 'displayed' less grandly. Never mind the view!

North Riding and Antrim glens
1950-1974 (2010)

§

light flares beyond only its own sake
tops of fells before sunrise's rake
still summer days the first rocks to bake
Eyes of the hawk sunken, hooded, yet darken
as with age, lighten with the red quartz. sharpen,
pupils open, bloomed to their quarry's markings:
the best optics evolved, detail beyond
beneath, between to which we cannot respond.
A glimpse all we usually get of them
before they are gone; even the 'slow' harrier
in disdain or indifference, never in ignorance…

Marsh Hawks. Hawk Mountain on Kittatinny Ridges

Appalachians pattern repeat ridges
rhythm parallel toward infinity
relieve Hercynian straining and tunes
old-mountain-building revealed its bones
old-timers know marsh hawks patrol below
the slope of the Hawk Mountain 'twitchers'
Across the grain of their expectancy
harriers go beneath the migrating-zones
of their hawk fellows 'herds'. Never *follow*!

Marsh Harrier Colorado – Hen Harrier, Lunds*

across maze or sage's haze-silvered lining
into the glare prairie-sun dry shining
spread shield changing tones of green
shadowed polished the arid-grasses' sheen
as over Helgill pastures less empty
white with earth if flower in '80
gled led words for your hour in the dignity
the Argus butterfly would come "serendipity"
as through our Greystead window in '83

* *that the Eden's source*

§

Harrier, not of the bare rockstrow
not of the deserts, above or below,
not of the limits, or of any other;
not really of the margin, the tundra
but when we yet allow their remnant
like all the Other Despised, existent…
and, in our absence there, even exultant.

§

Over Baysdale's Moss and Uswayford's
a wide-wavering flight we waved at
song more than larks'
of the silence of air
wandering arcs
we wondered at:
wintering hawks!
Soon we looked down upon
harrier roost; a coven.
Darkness part of it.
"Larking; nae profit!"

At a Nest, Cheviot

Blundered once onto a nest-site, its guards away
wondered where she had come from, though broad day
– bolder than other of our hill birds, I'd heard* –
hard her wings shuddered my hunched shoulders,
dodging grudge-buffets. She registered grasp after grasp.
Resisting each other. I still have the runes of her talons
amply; her bill's sharp-scalpel scars on my scalp…

Came away uneasy, in an even-deeper silence
– quiet had been this ('troll', I called her) violence
until Coquet springs reassessed themselves, now the Till
sang, for all the Distance, Time and space stood still.

1974

*Kenneth Richmond

§

There, over your hill, where I came 'nervier'
for, they are rarer now, merlin and harrier
of course there waves for us yet, boys' will savours
stilled the winds within, for the land is emptier
and I visit you this way, hoping for their favours!
We know they also must hold to their wierrd
their howes on the fell we learned to love well
and never found them empty of all but smell
of the moss and heather stirring, as once we feared!
The magic doesn't happen every time, for the barrier
between us is as between merlin, say, and harrier…

§

one for which, for once,
one doesn't have to be so quick
to see the diagnostics – oh, how slick;
the harrier's 'slow', whereas the falcon's quick…
glimpses are all that's given; the response
must be as theirs, as accurate
for us to begin to negotiate.

*

Sudden lurch, veering as the fog bank's
mutation is peremptory to mist-shroud.
Lurking, looking like its tongue, uncannily
leaving the same fractures trailing cannily
harrier waves in like a bower of bracken
(once, indeed, as a Spectre of the Brocken
somewhere in the Rockies.) Here grass ranks
at seed-time part for him as they don't
for the mist fingers. Then all is in cloud
the space of time a wet cheek takes
to dry once the hill mist has passed by
these long warm dawns, this Swardill July,
and here we are waiting, as the hay makes

Swaledale 1956
2010

§

He extends limestone-pavement upland, we see
tireless traversing clint and grike, travertine
raised-bog, rushy heath, matgrass, windward and lee
heather grousemoor, intak, cottongrass, is 'Seldom-Seen'
molinia tussocks waving under his wings, madly
broad swales and rigg acknowledge the furrow
accustomed tack, foreign to that merlin's arrow!

*

Stroke after stroke swift swimmer seems slower
than the wanton gulls' close transects-over
mists swallow him, their wisps the less the rovers
he becomes steam off the cauldron, this April only
found him gone when the summer opened bony
transforming as he had differently each landform
slow burn of winter the breathing becks do not warm!

*

Coveys keep break-of-slope between him and them
using the dead ground as if they were the guerillas then
for their next move on a grassy high chessboard, when
he climbs like a falcon and they "go back" again
medley alarms he floats over, drops so sudden
closed-wings, but flurried flapping in the midst
of an emptiness he'd not thought could be 'amongst'!

for Brian Wallace
Easter 1960, Malham

§

graceful as wherever their display courting is
it's more buoyant on these airs of Keewaytin
than on the south-easterlies – more agile charms
then though they ride them also, and all else between
stormy nor'easters and rare balmy dead-calms.
Like others little-known, over-looked, of 'the few'...
Not one of those known many North-American
humming-birds to cranes, and even pelican
which boom, at you, loom come-on at you
even in those glimpses some only afford
with gross gulls close with their 'all-aboard'!

Washington State,
Olympic Peninsula 1973

§

It is in our minds' convenience to deceive
in an illusion easy to believe
like the gulls are on that breeze,
in as constant-motion as the trees.
That the harriers comb and quarter and traipse
interminably day's face of this landscape
– so then why are they not the more often seen?

The same minds sink into the easy lulls
– too many of them are mistaken for gulls
(and not only 'blue hawks' – the "expected" prevails
processing blue/white or immature hulls and sails
pass like distant ships waving grey-green sea
or lowland fields' whispering roots, wheat, barley
as if no hunter but kestrel had ever been...

Stainmore, 1960

One bird's plunge through it is not

A harrier's ability, like a raven's
to go on vanishing after he's gone;
of his invisibility on this prairie
he needs no self-coloured mist or cloud.
Misled by tones in the skies' immensity
– no other "hawk" so hunted, haunted by sun,
they bulk differently, and are 'loud' –
we, Benét, are dismissed so easily,
ourselves part of his mirage low-flying…
unsure whether he's truly gone, or lying…
too often leaves little for the memory
we hard-scrabble to establish between us
despite the, that unfamiliar sort of fear
one thing emerges and no meadowlarks sing
even from post-and-rail, the nest near.
But two miles on, the erupting prairie
is of what is once was, and of a sudden
comes that sensation we weakly call 'queer'
and before he floats into sight the 'thing' –
for it is palpable – *is*; that had us steer here.

(Blue Cloud Abbey,
for Benét Tvedten and the Abbot)

§

'non per color, ma per lume perverte' (*Paradiso*, x, Dante)

        shorn
off barley-tassels
red light reflected up
here wheat, there Indiana corn
warms her breast
        flying over so close
of his bigge beer
grain measure of him
who watches thirst
to match hairst
        only waiting to roast
"Mondamin, friend
of Man" reddens

        (she floats ripening fields)

§

Something of the ringtail's progress arrests, yet
her waveform goes on half-recognised only
in those dropped stitches of time by the men
on the hill who wouldn't have missed one pipit
any more than one of their flock at this gathering
and the more so for all the rhythm of silence
the unspoken heard clearly for none are lonely
on this wavelength through the day, but her presence
scarcely half awareness, for he's quartering

as we all 'express' things of which we know nothing
the direct line to 'knowledge' through innocence;
whether we are heard by anyone taking notice.
Listen, the words have inner reckoning
echoing the inner arbiter of sense.

Words and worldview ever as mean –
his collie has seen it all before
is on his chin across crossed paws…
ringtail passes otherwise unseen.

Bilsdale Mid Cable 1954

Seeming animate cottongrass blows

glow-fluttering ghost-dance, daylight or moonlight
slow hovering over the spot into dusk and beyond
see s'ta (dye see) they fly waving chains, silver-white
up and down and around tussocks rusting with season
like larks' and pipits' ladder songs; my sister
things will o'the wisps of her Texas bayoux,
picks up wings the bats' strew as they flew;
we calculate over a hundred battlefield dead

* * *

some no doubt to birds; daw, merlin, lark
pipits with powder on their faces
a kestrel coming-on when it's almost dark
and yet the stronger image of those places
for her as for me, cottongrass head tossing dances
head-turning the more as light faded. Last there
where their ranks were richest forcing our glances
and spirits with them, hypnotic disordered stir
long after the ghost swift moths seemed fled.

with Jean   1975

§

A Blue-Hawk from the blackest hill comes on
his badge of long black fingerfeathers newly shone
by the wet; raven proclaims him prince among hawks,
all-black raven in deference hardly croaks, but squawks…
their cutting-edge of day a sharp wind and a snell
hones the edge of my bivouac ledge high on the fell
– all of the squall-clouds engendered, not 'sent'

*

Not presented; not, not to be 'a moment's ornament'
a grace, graces, for himself, where the black wind tears the bent
set in its place, weather its own jewel, as his strokes
not 'just for me' divide grey mist curtains of thick rokes.
Shepherd John, later, had gleaned of a phylogeny
"nay, he's mebbe nut an errn, himsell
but an errn must have be'n his fayther, ye see?"

(errn: the wide winged Grey Heron)

§

Scrolling silver shaken off stiffer fern fronds
rolling in a progress, snaking crests glitter bonds
trolling not trawling, fishing net drawn shorter
tauter as if with rumbling hydraulics of water
tumbling around she subtends from each shoulder
hunting her bounds and almost under each boulder
blunt wings' work; tips flicking to raise to the flush
young rabbits' panic or wader chick prey, at a rush;
quartering so low she comes on ahead of her shadow
goes on without breaking rhythm, though it may slow,
hundreds of wing-aching passes a day; success or no.

with R. Goncarczyk, Northumberland 1981

80

§

Scarps break out as limestone energies spend
she works limb to limb, urges round each bend
in the outcrop, hidden clints and grykes, former dykes,
up the face of the wind and fell, long seamed sikes.

Un-noticed, he has come from behind us as we ride
later, against the Helm wind up switchback Hartside
all torque held back but for the Morini single,
vibration damped but for the wind, so a tingle
affects you just as this gives; your first harrier
as silver-blue as the machine, our slim carrier
each wheels away, peels off for the next corner…

with F. Presley

§

See how with what John Clare calls a 'higgling tug'
seemingly gentle yet quick and firm enough
disembowels in usually one string all the stuff
from gizzard to cloaca, some birds swallow some up
but I've not seen harriers – with the meticulous
of the falcons leaving these delicacies
for any scavengers, even to shrews and wrens
at the gleds' feeding-tables soon after them
before autolycan jackdaws, crows and gulls,
who range these fells just too much as they please
to help clear up before the great black slug!

§

she flies the envelope of light the artists also seek
though they represent her, if they have seen her by a weak
vee or many vees, as if their skies had to have gulls
like this, or crows or pigeons…   Yet she sculls
ever in dihedral, more evidently purposefully than they
and the more gracefully using the whole column all the way
the length of the cloud-rifts ray, their tangent of the hand:
from the Consett Ironworks the perpendiculars rise
– skies belching clouds of their own, spreading reddening sore eyes
hilltop towers surprise as Tuscan towns' she also flies
in sight of not indifferent to because, at least; they shift the wind
and trim her sails and bring me the thrifty cargo glimpse spinned
down the years from other blast furnaces; Cargo Fleet, Indiana and
Russia: but rarely the Durham upland's sense of territory spanned

1980, 1990

§

Dry old birch leaves in his greaves tangled
tell he has taken his spell at the young ones.
Spins into his lower case taking up hanks to swell;
his swing showing me unappreciated 'woodland'
linking Wordsworth's 'little lines' – sap and blood lines
wych-elm and birch, rowan and rose briar – grand
sweeps of fell side thorns stunt up on the fell
ash trees whitened still whins sharpen spikes.
An hour later he nears, burden dangling.

'Ringtail' Harrier

earth close and resisting passage
pitching within the stiff stubble
thistle-bristles and frass of ages
summer gone and this its rubble
combing with light rays she comes
bringing the darkest of shadows
systematically, to each yard some
fresh colour and contrast below
her buoyant belly, resonant wings
transparent from where I lie unseen
under her line between Broad Ings
looking down with her on Seave Green
storing vignettes for the prosing days
away from both our wandering ways!

Bilsdale October 1956
(revised 2010)

§

A curlew's weakly resistance as at a distance
curtailed soon in a security of both talons
suffocated as easily as by a weasel
struggles contributing surely to the efficient
speed of despatch at the nip at the atlas
the curlew's neck extended for execution
and the tumbril; decapitated for flight hence –
long, open, decurved bill nuisance and hindrance
weight and bulk uneasy for a gled to manage

for Brian Wallace, at Scarth Gap, Newlands, 1959

§

Though a bird of our uplands it's the still more secure
the more fashionable, nobler species of raptor, I'm sure.
The peregrines advertised their presence more boldly
before their decline (by pollution) after about 195
in particular the territorial calling of tiercels who
like a massively amplified marshtit call the "pitcheoo"
rings out, echoes off the cliffs over the fells or quarry

some harriers seem to have learned to display more modestly
than they were used to do; the sky-dancing can be missed
as the goshawks' high spring display can be these days
perhaps unexpectedly early in the season; always perhaps elusive
these great hawks can be inconspicuous and reclusive
and I've known seasoned birdwatchers, not too familiar
with them, mistake the blackbacked gulls for the harrier
over those moor lands where the lesser blackbacks nest nowadays
and, as often, the buzzards with their ample soaring ways.
When a glimpse of a bird in cloud is all you'll often see
the "most likely" diagnosis often serves, but not for me…

§

Not high enough to be grey against the blue, a 'blue-hawk'
hardly disturbing the place's hidden-ness, or rim
comes out of the cutting itself unseen except from the line;
a black cross across then grey, gliding fine,
a robber-fly out of a turned-up high hat-brim
not the sudden-ness of a jump, a lift but also a stalk.
(Robber-flies, like dragon flies, are hunters like him)

North of the Prairie Provinces

she's un-noticed against the tundra brown
her pattern shrub stems, earth-patterns
ancient Caledonian mountains shattered
Canadian-Shield ground-down
her kind not by water – the Voyageur –
by earth – also knows the clues she needs,
minerals exposed, no less than birds
listen for echoes Highland, Hebrides
Shetland, Norway Fjells, Fjords towards
(not because we are told they are there
– from the other learning, the un-heard)
'Trust in nature' the sachem told, 'Be bold.'
The harrier-bird leads on a sense of occasion
(the carrion-bird cover after) if we follow-on
details of her survey can purvey experience
sequences repeated sense of sequence is
here she has muted precisely on a boulder
or bare ground from a height, Such markers show up white
and she seems to follow them tomorrow even if we do
and are in fog or white-out as if she once knew
though the ground is so much less featureless for her
being signatures and outcrops, traplines, constant care.

We are how/had not, have not, heard about...

I look at the bird and only slowly over the years see it
who has seen me from the first, even the first such bird as this is;
blue-hawk, cock-hen harrier, in full-plumaged beauty
improbable to expect, as is any surpassing of the textbook
scientific portrait (of an ideal) or any artist's ideal either,
(not the same ideals, but each short of strength as is my duty
looking into my eyes looking at last into, or at, his eyes

§

Bellini's landscapes are geometry alive
any bird flying-up puts the vertical in
essentially – horizontal pictures, to strive
after what the bird had, a balance of rhythm.

Must the naturalist try to give form
to the only – apparent 'chaos of nature'
or is he finding forms already there, warm
from creation, Billy* said; cold only to scorn
as the harrier is shown to work to a formula?

Her movements are *partly* controlled by the landforms
as course, but how and why and *does* she *conform*
only, and does this benefit the hunter at all?
The Northern 'passion' for nature, unlike Poussin's
be for control by reason by way of scepticism
no different from that of this my cousin*
each of us to become 'scientific' from that same passion…

* *a juvenile climbing-companion*

§

Harriers are good birds for the young to espy
easier to pluck out of the air
than those so elusively here and there
at speeds defying the eye…

even their cruising is at times elusive –
but there's good reason for every move they fly
they know where the crops of rodents thrive
get to know every tussock, rush or siv
over miles, if they are to stay alive…

Ringtail Reveals

great to live in the presence of the unknown,
unknowable, be a moment of your time sown
prodigally on these hills just to be so blown,
pelted, showing eventually where it is worth to go
prospecting for frogs, for voles, for ground – nests so
hidden here, by scanning as she does, the birds below
as good as old Harry's guess – the local 'hob (an elf) –
outcropped them along to Middle Limestone's long shelf.
(because they fmd me) I can find the grouse myself…

§

wavy-hair grass coronas flexing over the heathers
and a harrier benefitting from the neglect of this heathland
even to the extent of the autumn colouring of the tall grass
in ochres and old-golds and browns broken into her plumage,
rare ringtails remain a few for the banished goshawks and buzzards.
In years of visiting regularly on research we saw only several harriers;
a few of the Montagu's and only one pair nesting, in a great acreage
left by the great Vales of York our Mowbray glaciers, Pickering Lake
yet amongst the memories stemming from storm and shimmer
from the pulsings of adder and lizard ribcages in that sun
to the popping of broom flopping of lapwings all the summer
and the rhythm of "gled and fuckwind" when these had gone

For Susan, Sheila, Peter and Joe, 'Fuckwind' – local name for kestrel!)

§

blue, white and yellow
bluets and Johnny-jump-ups bellow
early-spring Texas prairie slows
followed by sedges, onions   pussy-toes
anemones and wood sorrels as at home
– not our acid woods but an acid loam
snow-geese over between the Bay and grazing
and a levee-patrol of a single marsh-hawk
pulses a vein and waves a plucked greenhead stalk…

near Brownwood, Texas – March 1989

§

ripples that don't stand out
against those all round
in the smooth waves of grass
sussurating cycles cross and pass
cold-steel-blue scythe of February ground
fooling a way through drumlin – fields
blue-hawk twin-screw sickle wields
(Nothing… but as the farmer has said; 'there's always a stretch of fields
     up ahead')

Cold Fell 1972

§

to assist us is parallax of the beat hypnotic
as herons shadow the pool with wider wings still
calculating against current and refraction for the bill;
anticipation like that guides the harrier's acrobatic
between the wave crests onto the one young rabbit
exposed that split-second, calm air near the earth –
speculate on scent if you must, as an assist;
what harrier smells – for me – for what it is worth…

§

We don't trust memory but we do trust the hill.
It started unexpected as fun often will
from finding a pluck-post remains of Stock Dove
 somewhere in the squall-clouds up above
Blue Row, Rookhope, Weardale
with Brian Latham, sent there by Hale
(Bill Hale) to see the mine and count waders
the late spring of nineteen-sixty-four
before Hierro and Gomera, just before;
found a harrier's nest here, felt invaders
guilty of disturbance, but took photographs.
He gave us the full De-Brief (short of polygraphs!)
– Reg Wagstaffe believed they were Montagu's
his wisdom not to refute or refuse…

(2005)

§

Following swales linking field to field,
meadow to pasture; faster there
bumble bees fumbling much more
than grey harrier prospecting at the Shield.*
Clanking heron cranks past, over
too big with his echo too big for a true rover
like harrier, and ever the first to yield...

(*Shield: shieling)

§

Formerly on traditionally-managed haughland
just as the harriers have, much declined
but didn't we see them at Elsdon, Eglingham?
we were above; the Tarset below and bright-lined
when her 'old-timer's' eye turned to me bright
with what was not what I call the light
from the birds of prey, glimpsed in flight
from her Reenes Farm, hill over Bellingham
no, the harrier had caught her eye, but the white
in the greensward on the fell by Sunday-sight
the little white orchis *Pseudorchis alba*
now inseparable from her own remaining aura

for Brenda Richardson, deceased (2005)

§

Randomly of all her snapshots, we supposed
repeatedly came up similar assemblage –
form of a flying cross, the 'bird' convention
appearing at the edge of her collage.

Girl from the coastal colliery village
– you know, close-built colliery rows
came upon us as we watched for the harrier
as if she arose as the bird's dihedral

Years later she apparently chose
us, of all the folk in the cathedral
at Durham, stood as if expected there
at Cuthbert's tomb under colours' rampage

And she floats again, substantial mote
we had come to stand beside her; little room
for anyone else to listen and not to stare;
had we seen "the big hawk catch the stoat!"

Lighting up with the Rose behind the gloom
the year after Basil died she shone
at Sid Chaplin's memorial there
and "where has the lovely harrier gone?"

(with B.B.)

§

...now the wind her tormentor
rides, rises over the water, slinging hail
recoiling to a stinging. Though commentator
she does not yield her silence to hail
the watcher, nor even glance askance once
gliding noiseless on long gentle wing-sail
tail narrowed now to almost a long point

    she gives herself instead to an eddy
this line storm has already made ready
for her passage over the lake, to steady
the cat-tails beneath her passing anoint.

Montana 1975

§

one who near the Rings of Thornborough cut the motor
stopped his tractor for a winged ring-tail harrier walking
weakly ahead. Not every farmer respects a hookbill's nature.
As best we could we bound up that wing and without talking
calmed the raptor with a splint of folded carton cardboard
we hoped would disintegrate as the wing healed, "oh good Lord" –
after she had flown we remembered we'd given the bird no jab
and we never saw her again, until one day his cab
– open those days – and it was all of eighteen months later
had a visitor when he returns there; she had returned to sit
with a lump in her humerus. And what lump in the throat greater?

§

for A. Watson, d. 2009

We went silently through the cemetery
watched over the river from its dyke boundary
for coming our way, the big bird of prey.
"Surely not a buzzard" I heard you gently say
grey as the reeds seemed, glazed at noon-day
waving eloquence along the breeze's reverie.

Third of your surname to spare me, rare tarriers,
time with me to watch marsh-harriers and hen-harriers
no mirage of the heat that day, no glimpsed falcon
or hawk but a full-view study. No lordly peregrine
but a humble workman, though no feather out of trim
for nest and young; just a 'fetcher and carrier'…

Farming folk of spare words and rare sentiment
(the heartier for that) the expected presentiment
for the hunter; his efficiently taking the one bird
singing the song unfamiliar, as yet almost unheard *
sighing with the reed grass for another not spared.
You were also, for once, lost in contentment.

* *Sedge-warbler*

§

The body steady, level whether rowing along or gliding
Could there be a better design for surveying widely
from moderate height, a true wide-angle vision
and forward and downward concentrated hearing.
But has anyone yet measured, assessed the precious
each sense offers, linked to buoyancy and steering
we marvel at in the harrier's slow-flying action?

Harrier of Storms

grass lands over and little-swards under
lash and quiver, gloss and shimmer
on the coming line-storm's change of weather,
set up a rocking motion in the heather

as below we'd watched change lay down wind rows
shifting partridge coveys, combing tallgrass meadows;
here new-hatched grouse chicks keep their cover –
as when her shadow like thunder-threat passes over

but now the buffets bend some stems near double
parting the swathes, and the hay's in trouble
yet there is always a further stretch ahead.
Inside the laithe, lifting our sweetgrass bed

between the dales the upland seethes
to its different tunes and changing tones
following each other under *two* shift wreaths,
revealing underlying limestone bones…

presence, sudden from beyond the cragline
a dark opening against the grey-white shine
as the 'burgomaster' gull sails over harbour, beach
almost metallic, and silver glinting underneath

Every bird in our view is now out of sight
even the 'daws and crows on the cut fields;
the harrier patrols against the light
with the wind and at minimum speed…

Two partridges are detached from their covey, 'sunning';
'look outs' at the dykeside, and the cut-edge,
but one has not taken cover, and is running –
and, just in time, gets under a thruff-stone's ledge…

Some Harrier Regular Diets

*(NB Some North American English names for rodents were initiated
in Lees-Smith and Simms' provisional Key-List of 1979)*

Like almost every predator in the temperate zones today
earthworms form part of their food, often that of their prey…
From examination of food remains left at many a plucking-post,
roost, nest-site and from castings-analysis they eat rodents most
(except on a few moorlands with grouse and other smaller birds):
that they are full of shredded grass and other leaves
seeds and earthnut protein; full as guns, little sheaves
is as apparent from harrier castings as from leavings
on their picnic tables in the pastures, their fellside groovings.

*

If I can catch them in their runways, not needing traps,
easily as lemmings or pikas, these cold snaps
kestrels and stoats and weasels and anyone else also can;
oval food-parcels: as tasty, surely, to early man
– as I have found, roasted; as they warm this harrier roost

*

Plains pocket-gopher, other pocket-gophers, 'pocket-mice';
longimembris, hispidus, and a range of the Kangaroo mice
and of Kangaroo rats and of harvest mice and *Peromyscus* mice
Sitka mice, Canyon mice, Deer mice, and Difficult mice
Plains woodrat, other woodrats, hamsters, many kinds of lemming
not forgetting in both old and New Worlds *sibiricus* Brown Lemming
and at least eight species of the at least seventy species of voles
including our familiar Bank, Field, 'Water', pine, Orkney, root, and
        prairie voles…

7,000'-1,000' Absarok, and Alston Moor, for example.

Ringtail

Spread out for her; a score for her movement or
ours; the corpus of the horizon rises and falls
Cleveland's backcloth escarpments in rank for her.
What in this corner of the North are not called fells
Odinsberry, Easting, Bottonheed, Urra, Hasty Bank,
Cringle, Cold Moor, Scarthmoor, Scugdaleheed, Carlton Bank
reflected in her sweeps of their dependent becks and stells.

we climb, she with us, their stair and their wind stint
in our faces, sheltered of westerlies, southwesterlies
where we collect bilberries she's working the skerries, scars
the peathags the old trods, the former quarries
for families of voles, pipits, peewits, moles
below the acid ground, and then upon it
lizards and grasshoppers, beetles and moths

billies full we children tire, stretch out in satisfaction
purple-stained, and strained to the further expectation
rarely missed of the kestrel there on station
over the hill-gate, our way back down to staggarth
and dark kitchen, Stitching the banks together
into the evening also goes but a lone harrier
starting the heart with the at last heather weather

§

the harrier on the worn old milestone as regular
this winter as she walked that way often (and in great age)
I'd wanted her to see for herself, not as passenger
but on foot herself, "sauntering" alone, and to engage
not be shown. From a distance I saw the blue hawk arise
to full height on long legs. Her movement of "such a surprise
but I didn't stop, I started laughing, softly you know
and the beautiful bird 'set' back down. Why didn't it go?"
She had kept going, not staring at it, though "so bonny."
The way to see things is through being so free to do so,
The road is narrow. "Oh, I've seen them *before,* you know!"

for Bessie Armstrong
Alston Moor 1995

§

Curtains of hill fog cross the slopes athwart
besetting the mind then the eye with uncertainties
closing us down to nearer perhaps what we are
and halfway-scarfs tantalising possibilities
as when waking bleary 'in the midst of sleep'
unaware of time having been passing in the dark
this long belt of light fog girdling the near steep
then the eye plucks a rhythm's stuttering start
for the harrier hunts here as he can hunt in cover
hardly seen, weaving elusively, insubstantially
revealing a broken graph of the contours other
than the map offers, and the bog we are told to fear
with the enlarging lens of the mist discover
before all perception, perspective, can disappear…

South Lanarkshire 1972

Bewcastle 'Wastes' and Alston Moor

(the same blue hawk, weeks apart*)

Now that the trees are where they were saplings
seedlings planted by displaced persons, Poles;
the long-wings have no room for flapping
the forests offer too few birds and voles
so the cockbird's gone, seen at the Tyne Gap
fortuitously (for all the hours spent there alone
over fifty years then) – a very small cock harrier
in an intermediate plumage; weathered-stone
coloured mantle, and greaves scarred like a warrior

and the bird goes slowly along the road,
yes; past your home, asking to be followed
easily, for it keeps bobbing along the road
you can walk, say to the Rushy Field Hollow
where the bird turns aside over the Grass of Parnassus
and then resumes progress above the road below
when you have even got a little ahead of the harrier
and now he is weaving toward further pastures
(Nattrass's) where we make wading-bird censuses

*confirmed when the bird was found dead beside the road a few days later

§

He announces himself, teetering
peat-hag off this high blanket-bog
to where I watch a cuckoo-squab squat,
ugly and ungainly, gaping
at little pipits' frantic fuss
feeding their demanding monster blob
even rowanwood's cheeky chaffinches
are drawn, to fetch leather jackets –
who can ignore hungry infants?

Even says HE IS, that sort of squawk
both meek and urgent, pleading the cause
of the earl, though clad in such rags!
And the more sharply as he nears
he complains, hysteric, insistent,
I plead he is drawing his parent.
I am well enough hidden from them all
for *them* to tend *theirs*, his to recall *him*
to that one harrier's nest for miles…

He is what he will be, but ragbag
ridiculous; half-furled flags and down,
wings too clumsy even for balance,
legs too long, feet too big for tussocks;
yet to proceed, with his race's dignity
stilts through the rushes, shuffling
tumbling, so he keeps disappearing
dinosaur over old *Equisetes*:
aristocrat of the air next week!

(juvenile hen harrier)
North Pennines '06

§

Moving out there – the sea of tawny grass breaches
urge, surge or wave of it reaches us
a change of tide to reluctant beaches
face in a cowl facing down, a floating grace
monastic at prayer in progress blessing place
a notion over prairie no other can trace
no other surveyor now the wolf and bison gone

*

unless this is the shape-changed challenger
coming-on with the breeze at twelve/fourteen miles an hour
from horizon to beyond horizon once forever
solitary where once the great herds rolling onward
put up the hoppers for her gophers and voles toward
more than sufficiency; efficient system's reward

*

the child out with me from the reservation
knows her better than I do, to a bird-totem
put another child to sleep just by watching them
wind in grasses crooning as gently as by lullaby;
my grandmother waiting for pheasants over high*
rocking me until sleep, and "the bairn put by"
the shock is not empty once the marsh-hawk's gone on.

* to note where they roosted, in which tree tops, for poaching in the dark

The Goshawk / Harrier Incidents of Nov '09

with Tom Pickard

One after the other sweep the Tyne pastures;
do they hope to raise the same rabbit
and nab it; or make-do each with a pipit?
Swooping magnificent, each out of cover
gled and then goshawk recalled those days after
the glide precision of the one, the dash of the other,
A gled, next day, flew over up the Tipalt;
no cover, so hovering and quartering
plunged as an osprey on a vole swimming –
ahead of watervole – gone, a wake rippled…
The same tossing of your wings –
there's no life without stings –
raises the ash and opens its leaves
and whatever the new vicar believes…

Harrier Over

Whole hill kicks into motion, as its molehills
are all rabbits; scores of scattering daft wills;
scuts and ears up, heads jerk tense, hesitate,
fur flies off green-again, bitten-down turf, spills
levelled pasture again. Were they all sleeping late?
Devil-may-care, a young buck rises on his tail
to be knocked over unconscious of the gled's long flail…

North Redesdale 1982

Katharine MacGregor — of The Sneep, Tarset

She said, graceful lady of wisdom, 'they will be back'
this is their land, especially so before the forestry;
Gleedlees their pastures, hunted Bimmer (when I was a boy)
Ridley Shiel an egg laid as bright as moontrack
good sense since of the likes of Wilson, McCracken...

there we were, me more trouble to the sheep,
each prospecting a place to live near Sneep.
Blackburn Common, the Tarret, and the Dargues Hope
and led by big huntring Kestrel from Woodhead

fell in with a harrier that spring which,*
cockbird, forced our kestrel into the ditch
toward Heathery Hill, and later, perhaps
killed her by Pit Houses, pierced corpse
not scavenged, but post mortemed; instead of course...

(1990)

* (dec. March 14th 2010
Hexham Hospital, at 88)

* Hen Harrier tried to nest some seasons
I watched them there, by Tarset and Tarret.

§

Jan 20th, 2005

'Ringtail' Harrier again, worked from the back bedroom
carrying a pheasant minus wings, longitudinally
from the direction of the little pine Knoll
into the wood edge; fierce wind most of the day

Feb 7th, 2005

'Ringtail' hunting, Crossgill to Tynehead west side
in intermittent sunshine from 7 am. until 10
puts up blackgame: 13, 4 and 11 toward Dorthgill,
Raven 4, go away soon. Fieldfare 18+70+8 and more off Hill House
(misses one straggler very near in 4 attempts to fly down, low partridges
grab from just below, left foot.
On to Study Area: where seen to land as usual and still, 20 minutes)

April 14th, 2005

in swirling snow an hour ago
our 'ringtail' on the nor-easter's scour…
Took by surprise (my surprise) a blackhead gull
over by the White Sike 'reservoir'
but left most of it to the 'crows'…

Adder Kill

Sudden, our pace does slacken;
sullen, there is the bracken
where Kate lifts her skirt high
he pulses with the bared rhizome
we both pulled on to get up by
(the roots (which) are devouring the hill
– once sweet sheepwalk, cattle-terraced
before he came (also) and we couldn't kill
him or wreck his rusty fronds of a home).

We reckon him wick, yet he seems too still
find his skull crushed, his tension a dream;
we waited hidden, and, bidden at last
the blue-hawk returned; that had silken gleam
glimpsed at (the) hill fort against the overcast.

*

Dennis and I on Cross Fell
are lifting another harrier
under horizon's mirage
off blanket-bog and long swell;
cadence breaks the barrier
cryptic, tonal otherwise.
Hot air, we can smell
thyme's, violet's, no surprise.
Before the gale's strength she flies…

Dennis and I, under spell –
all senses grace harrier
windpulse infer, deliver.
If we can't come near her,
what can be told we can tell!

for Dennis Currah

§

Wind in the thistles whistled
subsong to the gold-finches'
sibilance. This Birdseye sward
is past its primroses hoard:
harriers flying below the benches...
Did they teach the crows to do so
or learn from watching *them*?
Some gullies seem to be *theirs*,
a better security than nothing.

*

Wind deters, in the interests of music
a few who came despite the rain
and you have the respite for life again
– the nesting place as yet undiscovered,
the grouse fallen silent above the gill
because you hunt away, like the fox
and, like him, are not seen often enough
even by the sentinel curlews circling above
– but your numbers will not recover
from such a slender base on this hill,
and too few like it your silent music fill.

The Hieratic Marsh Hawk (Gaudier)

for Ezra Pound, 1978

The Dead or Undead circulating around forever
somewhere near enough that strand once of the harrier,
silly at the end of that field they call Piccadilly
which, like Broadway you once had prospected in those frilly
panties just-showing as pretty undercarriage feathers
seasonally discarded over hayfields and heather.

Not yet, monuments to the Architect and Milliner
for the dead monument is to dead Eros principle
who had to die for the distillation of the nation
who, dead, think he is alive somehow, somewhere in them
whilst this proud Harrier image lives on in participle.
For the land was his, The Peoples', in their occupation
who are still more alive, being 'gone', than our civilisation
and reappear, like him, not as ghosts, when the town moves on
ironworks decay, and their spoil heaps for prey grown-over
Gary, Indiana, will be seen yet and in London
just as the undead, dead of its nitrate rises the clover
willingly, the living return to live their dominion.

(The ubiquitous North American Marsh Harrier is the same species,
with the same lifestyle, save for details of course, as the Hen Harrier)

§

(They call it pair-bonding, this high-air fondling)

wider than I can see
his orbit sails me,
rings with hail stinging
corbelling larks' singing
over pipits' riddle-me-ree
this silent far-slinging
perspectiving morning.

breath lost to the one
then the other phenomenon
is found to make the gill
we can hide in. keep still,
as guilty, me and Alan
as, singing, full of beer
we'd run late, for the bus.
That same kind of fear
looks up at the above-us
food-pass between
these seldom-seen.

(nest-site, North Pennines, May 2006)

§

September 20, 1997 with Michael, Ringtail above Dentdale
(after watching Mountain Ringlets further west, one of *those* days?)
waltzing, walking the turf, close as the warm haze
collected a hatch of crane flies, not lifting us her gaze...

November 18, 1997 Ringtail harrier onto immature grey hen
watched, seconds only, from the Morini, by that long sken
which will one day have me tumbled in the dyke agen!
miles on of Westmorland I couldn't quite see
what in the wet Blue-hawk picked up off grey scree...

They didn't stay to nest...

Just arrived on the fell cock ringousels' carousel
of last-season's nest-site tossing in the squall
distort broadcast each reveille rivalling call
their history in larches lurch toward ecstasies
but the cock hen-harrier will take them all...
blue gap just big enough that they had come through
tup-hole in cloud-cover westerlies skewed-up
enlarging for the blue-hawk's corkscrew display
carrying one of them, too light after journeying
for the ringtail to catch in the pass, gust blew
shuttlecock between them she missed gathering

* * *

each of the others, weary, were taken that day
emaciated beauties, only acid-flush to sup
a few dried rowanberries, a few spiders in the dyke
and the gled back for each one, and not to stay
to tear the best breast meat, but to carry away
high-diving silver longwings, tips dipped in ink
as old Alan would say, leaving them his mowdies
out on their hills on the pasture, cursing the greedy
crows; "fetched a gun if he'd stopped to think!"
Seeing only her head over the heather, main spectator
in my view up the fell – a failed negotiator...

for Alan Watson
8 / 9th April 2008

Their signature

Shrouded witches in dull shawls
they are still constellation
Seven Sisters of the Pleiades
assembled at roost in company
standing about under stars
at least three of them sisters
from all points of the compass
to this shoulder-high cover;
one of them shuffles like the comet
wobbling in air turbulence, a progress
every one of them one-eye watching her.

(Spirit)

of the spirit of place
as words are daughters of earth
     as light is, of the air
nomads as 'The People', who were
these harriers still are
     and as their race
wander over its face forever

Hen Harrier Defiance

bolt from the blue ahead of the storm
she rises across my path, a challenging cross
blunt-headed, wings spread black against the sun
a warning sign she's keeping her passion warm
her hover shuddering in sudden emotion
whilst a surge spreads beyond under her curse
panics of grouse scoom just before they lift
away over the heather, rocketing so low at first
peregrine might be deterred; they get height because of *harrier*
dwindle into distance, their disturbance heat wave
un-nerves; I am not brave as she is brave!

Co. Durham, 1969

Ecker Secker Bank, Cautley

Howgill harrier quarters wicket to wicket
hollow to hollow mellow in rounded hills
repeating the contours of her clutch of eggs,
she floats out of sight into the beck below
but shows up the other bank and we cannot follow –
bowled by the 'arm ball' she shares with the wind.

Watching their display-flights had been to feel the spin
of the ball we all lose in the glare off the turf
her guile in flight quickens the blood we are in–
red, as you said, cricket balls help boys to the edge
of self, some to manhood, dun sheens the sedge,
and after school the hills' cadence, hawks dance.

for Robin Walton at Sedbergh School, 1999

§

because he comes out of fens
'moor', 'marsh', 'bog' also afford
interchangeable tokens
in the Northern word-hoard
cursed is any bill curved –
and not only amongst us men
we watched a gled badly served
by his intended hen bird
sword-hatred a sworn kindred
an inevitable dread
of death lurking in fen fog
as Grendel from his bog…
Hen harriers are often polygamous;
he was killed by turned up talons

summer-high clouds and the rain
visible silver curtains, caught up again
by shifts of wind, so not reaching the ground
– hen harrier featherdown fluttering around –
nothing in these skies no longer seems strange
a stage of drama soon spreads the Cross Fell range
when things seem familiar, predictable
expect the unexpected and the unpredictable.

1971

§

Out of hill mist as often before
looming larger than life, as often before
seeming darkened, distressed, talons clenched.
Where the birch has fallen clean across the burn
for her to perch on, I'm hidden near to learn;
how unlikely that water should be her friend,
revelling in such swift company to send
spray from long wings lashing the surface,
she lunged from her perch and, nothing precious,
she's weltering water to where larches lurch
and low alders arch over, and I am drenched...

Keeping his shadow close to himself
close behind and under not to scare the voles
flies the hollow mine-pond overflow for the hushes
then the deeply incised burnhead where the spring gushes
he follows the glacial overflow channels carefully
in the same discipline, slowly to inspect all the rushes
and stroking those round the margins of the swalleys
widdershins – his shadow impinging their holes
and the frogs explode inwards in sudden volleys

and he shakes himself away, a sodden elf
looking sideways over his ruff at me, ruefully?

§

Close the 'keeper showed me how close
she passes between old sheep, "near skinned",
as nearly as the grasses sweep under the wind
not noticed, apparently, by some of them – so
that where she rises at the end of her pass to turn
her string of pearls deceives the oncoming hare
but takes a decisive swipe at a surprised snipe.

Why Rising Hen Harrier

What does his circling say, and why?
(wing tips dipped in India ink)
he *can* write across the sky.
Why rise so high that we blink
into the sun – can't be to try
his ardour, when April comes by
and a likely mate; that he tips a wink
and dives, in another blink of the eye
in case someone's watching, with a gun
whose idea of worshipping the same sun
is to bake himself pink at Torremolinos
then show himself off to some 'jolly girls' for fun?
here on our hills with stottie and Thermos
we think he means Himself, alone, why-aye!

Western Cheviots, Spring '79
with Bob and Lin
For Valda Trevlyn
and Mary Dawson, the pub at Biggar

§

At Carts Bog harrier plays on the baize
pocketing rabbits and voles only a little ahead
in Milky May light right over to his horizon
from just a few feet above it, a long true cue
and where he hasn't missed, a little round of red
before the kecks are up this new grass glaze
hesitates under his wing before its wind is rising.

May '03

§

Harrier over the barley field eases
mekkin its silversilk surface's breezes
shift its napp; stirring sheets of deceiving
giving and taking cloudshadows at great speed
(the only parallel I find, won't fit the need!).
Better I remember the polarisations
of crystals turning under the crossed nickols
illuminating the microscope's lit field;
one kaleid replaced instantly by another.
Bird cutting-in and out of its own dance
at each field's lands' turn, and often mid-ways
at once deathwhite, dynamic silver and dull greys
black wing-tips splaying, fingering the rays
as along the shaft of a tempered lance.

Askerton / Nichol forest
1998 with Tommy Elliott

§

...they've shifted their roost, and one and all
before the dripping-down is heard and increases
to fill the forest much heavier than leaf-fall
and the snow softens as it loosens, releases
off branch and bole, and dibbles into holes
and old snowloads tremble and tumble in spurts
spruce trees are seen to lift crowns and skirts
with relief of weight, and some of them 'create'
over noise of the river rising feet in hours of spate
one harrier is watching avalanches sink and fling
but none of them will still be here in the spring...

Harrier Taking Off Unobserved

Both of us now hours into our crouch on our haunches
light as an air in both senses, only the bird launches!

One glimpse of flight, in a moment's abstraction
in a devotion like in any calling, in hope, or expectation
which pattern is a song for a rare strong satisfaction
as the good thing of a poem if it is good enough
transfixes both sense of beauty for its sudden moment
and attention also fleeting if it is the right stuff

Concentration meets warmth, and the work starts fermentation;
emotion having set out a line, a landscape in motion.
So there is music in it and that, personal culmination
an apex not to be repeated, but a growing point
And then the pines beyond respond to the wind and wave
and with the shift the sun finds new shoots to anoint.

In front of Easby Black Plantation 1966

§

Cotman's Greta Bridge at a moment
of combination after Turner's contemplation
of High Force not far away, not silent
the blue hawk has sped downstream between them.
Neither seem to have caught any motion
as he has – shooting as if a hundred mile wind
the harrier's passage seemed to be thinned
under the bridge where Turner met Cotman;
shooting an arch just over the race of water
no faster, with air current, than an otter
spinning in its own eddy, then away steady.

§

one of those days the dew doesn't lift soon
under the roof of cloud sending out a full moon
day lightens only enough for the less-solid fog
to lift off most all but the high blanket-bog
still lifting black block spruce plantation
yet a sense of increasing light, slight revelation,
a little more, just, than we hope it must...

So that a little after the gloomy mid-day
some east-coast roke begins burning-away
and sudden the sodden cock hen harrier's grey
mantle, showing almost black is taking on slate
blue and scattering silver as if anxious and late,
he grooms – but not, not yet, 'for ultimate mate'
he tries wings only to dry them, and goes back to sleep

March 1970

§

"Not me, not me, but the wind flying through me"
and the harrier flying alongside the Triumph twin
using us sometimes to skim under the wind's skin,
Boggerah Mountains on the way to Cape Clear; we
use the break of slope as we've seen you do, elsewhere
glad that the storm is in our faces, we trust it there.
In both senses transient as us, see she moults a few feathers
– how can we transmit what seems to be given to us?
drawing on drawing or language as poor as this is!
ghostly this raptor is, has always seemed the most Irish
least observed, for all that she is almost unique, too lish
to be praised or pinned down. One haunted Cape Clear
that visit without being seen by the several ornithologists
on that small island then (including M.B.O.U.s, as Oxford Men).
How many pass for 'buzzards', anywhere? And I still fear
no-one else yet believes I found harrier castings in its fen
and on one of its Atlantic promontories. They're in my lists
(their contents) of thousands of hen-harrier digests!

§

over all these their ranges
into and out of their heather
Alan's wether sheep stream together
toward where he has their 'fother'.
Against their current, a stranger
I have to find 'behind the ranges'
(never two days the same) those changes
the harrier makes for the weather.

and find her there at her tether
stint miles wide, many miles long
like casting-off on stream after stream
the routine gives rise to some song –
scanning-horizons' scheme; closer the theme
to my rime the nearer, the more strong
the pattern, a matter of life and death
to her – to me, mere gaining my breath!

lose her in dead ground, but all's not lost
that's part of the oldest dyke she's just crossed
and may rest in the borran beyond, to see…
and I've dropped delighted onto one knee
out of her sight, at some jewelled fragment
the dew illumines at my feet that torment
of leather jackets and their daddy long legs together
a shining scarab, *Carabus* king of the heather!

§

light bounced off crystalline snow
and from *within* that soft crystalline
growing rosy for morning's threatening storm
gaining the top of the rise, and wanting to show
Mary coming-on below. Up its spine
and over, sensation of that sudden warm
of the heart at the art of the bird stalling so
slow, yet no detour around us. This carrier
has something for us; a note dropped by harrier
light blue and grey uniform clean cockbird goes
other snow-colours, counter shades yet shadowing
ahead of us careless; for indifference shows –
relaxed wing-caress, hardly a beat of wing
space and pace deceptive as befits the place
so to go overlooked to most (and no disgrace).
we who cannot follow more than moment
wonder at momentum, direction, the motion
echoes emotion, no need to ask what was meant.

Upper Teesdale

§

Brown, they huddle under distant thunderheads
cowled, haloed, ruffs stuck out, stiff as stuffed ikons
as the sun squeezes under clouds lights brighten peathag heads
and they respond with tartan plaids wrapped round, and liken
horizon's (for I'm deep in the heather) dead-tree-stumps
overtaken by the peat long ago, fossil, statuary…
Yes they are still essentially reptilian articulated lumps
– for all reptiles and birds have a relict mineral quality
inherent in bill and scales and talons, eye-rings, much other
not only as night comes on do they seem stones and litter
apparent as their parent stars and our mirages dither!

Harriers Ahead of Events

He comes off the limestone at gliding-on pace
ahead of the linestorm, ushering it in
as the eagle will, some falcons, the raven
less-so also wildfowl, those who don't need to chase
so that those living on the long-distance path
know better than 'living-dead' and their forecasts
(such learnt slow but sure – not much made by haste).
Thus the harrier pulls the curtain across
realises the sky, yet snaps at the fly
lumbering across his flightpath to get done
despite heavier air to roostground, and dry
and keep it dry under him, head hidden in ruff-boss
a shield (or a shorteared owl) lest the stun
of first, heaviest, drops from the darkening sky

The Pennine Way 1972

§

Upper South Tynedale to uppermost Teesdale
not quartering for prey, to skim the watershed
in prospecting flight, tacking into the gale
and out of it gliding; the mark of the gled!

Our rover flanks in his long-wing caress
golden plover flocks in near-breeding dress –
three fifty-one in splendid 'Arctic' colours,
forty more 'British' on separate pastures;
this passage of the harrier doesn't flush
more than a few, and even these don't rush
though *they* put up seven hundred loud fieldfares,
twenty oystercatchers, a cloud of redwings,
redshank and dunlin in little spurts and flares,
five hundred pewits, a pair of reed-buntings!

April 2003

Solway bivouac harrier

Parallelograms, rhombs of easy flight
repeated beats under lozenges of cloud
stirring stanzas summing reflecting light
have me humming your rhythms aloud
refrain at the turn of each run or round
using my shelter, a little raise of ground,
no helter-skelter rushing; a passing shadow
is not more deliberate, is less delineate:
energising as any oystercatcher crescendo
what this bird dances, not sings, is 'follow'
wherever meaningful patterns indicate.

1958/9

§

In swirling snow an hour ago
'our' ringtail on the nor-easter's scour
took to my surprise a "laughing" gull
ridibunda, Black-headed gull –
over by the White Sike 'reservoir';
mobbing by some six of the others
but left most of it to a lone crow.

I stumble across, unable
to begin to translate
her passage across the horizon
low in the sky, hardly clear of the ground,
so that she scarcely shows against the grey
and the motions of the waxing herbage
and of the air itself confuses, a mirage...

Alston Moor, April 15th 2005

121

Harriers at a Spring Roost

a coven of ringtails as if conjuring-up a cock bird
to mate with them: some males have a choice in polygamy
(in our abstraction). Indifferent, the coven members haven't heard
perhaps, seem careless as to his presence, or are just canny
of the silver, swinging, handsome cockbird over there
who has eyes not to see them but to catch the ranny
ahint the dyke he pommel-horses over, the more aware…

dull as the winter, as silent they are as ghouls
shrouded, stationary; but they could be blathering
amongst themselves *sotto voce* as they do over voles
and to their own young – hardly audible yet gathering
the morale in their chicks, and no doubt terrorising
rodents. Wind ruffles their flying, even in this calm
for it is their own wind their wings will be rising,
and the chicks know this song, also, keeps them from harm,
yet respond by 'freezing' when the heron comes over
or the buzzard, and we will call these things "instinct"
in our ignorance. Mystery deepens, whatever we think!

§

rattling her feathers like a ghost in the frost
which still coats the thruffs on the other side of
this dyke I work for lizards, out of sight of
her] stooped; not to deny her the beetles and spiders…
shuffles on her post reluctant at night's lost
calm, she's already flown-in seven miles of
glazed fell dazed by the moon careless of
gazing at us, me keeping shadow of outriders
of the jackdaw flock at point – they haven't crossed
my line (toward her and she's showing no profile)
hundreds making for the sheep feed
                                    at what cost
to hill farmers and the rest of nature. Scavenge
any life they will, often disdaining rich road kill
for the pipits' eggs, the peewits', insects, frogs,
any berries, fungi, seeds, larvae they'll see…
In this parish this winter to date (it's April,
lambing late; the 'keepers say they've shot hundreds)
she's knocked fifteen down herself in front of me…

§

There is no describing the prairie, even if you find it,
no just definition of *condition* by mere description)
but something happens in 'mind' or 'spirit', or in mind and spirit:
powerful impressions don't have to be precise, but *vision*.
The prairies put up the need, but then put up the barrier;
best at it are the 'hawks' (which are buzzards) and the harrier
they call 'Marsh Hawk' – our eloquent-flying familiar
flies even when little is left of the tall-grass prairie
– Big Blue-stem and Slew-grass the most grand species –
to seven feet tall and higher. Flown by the hen-harrier
at angles and heights he knows) we don't, what he sees…

Blue-stem Hills, Kansas, 1973

§

Grey cloudless rarely, but all the more welcome for it
they roll o'drums the snipe's and salutations pipits'
curlews lang coorlin calls, shy gowdies' plaints askance
sun comes up sudden full, over all this plateau at once
her High Pennines unbroken advance. We wait on his strength
no pussy-footing about with higher hills, few shadows measure their length
bar the tallest dykes, deepest gills, edges of the few plantations.

From yellow-line in the east only any clouds give him rest
until it's time to quickly redline under the scarp line to the west.
Morning; she's off her roost scooping up the light airs lifting then
at the height to discern in the heather the grouse pairs, cock and hen,
scorning the lordly peregrine's stooping hard out of the sun
she exercises dummy runs – no self-respecting falcon!
but picks up a vole almost casually, but my expectation.

Little acquainted with the higher reaches of the air
she's as careless of our concern for the concept of remoteness
– being a 'rarity' is the norm for a predator like her…
with all the time in the world relaxes flying, face muff unfurled
and sun's strength brings forth insects and blooms of her world
and turns the beams on her with all her 'reptilian ancestry' –
spreading across the dyke top a flop, for my easy theory!

with all day to measure, and marvel at its weather
and gainsay, in time, she's "as lazy as any buzzard"
glad at crack with the rare keeper here or a shepherd
unsurprised at the old Northern tales of green men The Wizard
of Abbotsford conjured, and Joe Wilson's Tales of the Borders.
She has her stints only the less regular than these wethers'
for her gifts of flight and sight –- but she's not free altogether…

Keeping an eye fixed on her, and my stride, is she laughing
at butterfly, stoat, cranefly, bee, moth I'm missing?
Yet she flies low and slow, so in my line of sight her ride
much of what else there is – is it pride? turns me aside
to name the insects before moving-on – for there she is still!
And when eye turns to sleep, with what does 'void' fill?
So her's has anchored, and buoyed, and answered my own will.

§

A few men and boys climbed up to share
with the bird these meltwater spillways
– scratting for a living as we were
her quartering using our ranging-poles
– our surveying summoning souls?

winter much more than summer courses
pondering Huntingtonian limitations
– intimations of moulding – forces...

before morning's pipits were astir
far above Colliers'-back settlements
in the view in our theodolite
(limitation of vision, content)
the lay of the land already in her sight
and grasp – she's solid will o'the wisp
grappling for our astonishment
boggart at cell of Father Postget
Minister to the Moors, the cusp
Christ's intake. Intake of wind, or breath...

(Surveying for glacial meltwater channels (1951)

Ringtail

– lengthening days she stravaigs
this sort of shore, spread stain-more
home-fells where I count nest-cells
cups of eggs in mossy floor
pigmented every shade
peats and plants and stains explore

    perhaps she's seen a hundredth of them all
    quartering the fell four hours or more
    and alarmed scores of nesters, a squall
    passing over with a few mock attacks, war
    has not been declared but she has selected
    one, 'the weak to go to the wall', elected.

fast from the dyke's blind approach she shouts
talons swinging forward with the momentum
and purpose in one, as she brakes on wing-roots
and pinion noisy at last, blasting continuum
grasping the gaudie fore-and-aft from behind.
The insect-hum resumes. The eggs are to find.

1958 (2009)

Davy Watson's Harrier

Baz and I once heard his skirl at far-away Troughenn;
If he's here, we stop for crack coming over the Carter
as we did yesterday on our way for cheese in Jedburgh
and get the 'Burns Season' colours with Mary and Ken
    But here the Tone is the zigzag crazy burns' career
    off the Redeswire and Whitemoss in hill-mist's linger
    and up from Catcleugh our course paralleled by a harrier
    when Dave shifts his plaid and points, whole body and finger
The bird comes on, perhaps triangulates by the Border Stone
and flies low up the Border Dyke as if reluctant for Scotland
seems taking an order from us to keep track along the Border;
still on the line as she passes out of sight over Deadwater
    And Davy is ready for bait and drink in Bonchester
    so we take him and after a mile, there's the bird again
    (or "one", as he said "identical")

On the Medicine Line

Weirder in evening shadows deepening than energetic badgers' emerging
palefaces' moonphases inserting than anything returning to a rookwood
the undergrowth they walk is in motion, stalk-legged wind rushed loose bush
doubt delivering this roost of marshhawks, forgive if we forget the first flush
of recognition, harriers out of usual context, alert as hares out of forms
shrouds shape changing and melting back into cover sudden as prairie-storms
not force off the hills but vortex ever the evening engendered by endless plains
the only unguarded frontier; save of course by the customs' men
is like all frontiers ignored, unknown to the real last frontier men
the sandhill cranes and the meadowlarks and longspurs and winter wren
where even the despised and shot-at marshhawk can come and come again

(the 49th parallel)

127

§

'Economic' forestry has spared this Border glen
– so far – though decimatad *its* black moor-hen
the "bubbly jock" black-cock; a national disgrace
and with it, of course, part of that sense of place
but increased the small birds and rodents there –
where merlins have nested "more than two hundred year"
– twenty already in my time, and *this* season…

this same day as the jill merlin has
she has turned her eggs, to prevent them
aborting of the embryo there
– the chick-to-be is already free and
maybe already aware of care
not constrained by the shell membranes
can the henbird sense what she cannot see?

Look round from these nests, sitka spruce tide knows no reversal!
Now, every hilltop awaits its crown of thorns –
our 'renewable utilities' on dilemma's horns;
yet again the substantial waits on the ephemeral
to know its fate in the futilities of 'techifashion'.
The worthies shake their heads over the curlew's decline,
the peewit's, the golden-plover's. Who's next in line?

§

like other carnivorous birds at the nest, harriers
anoint part of it and themselves with insect-repellent
as they bring in green fronds and mosses) disinfectant
we consider decoration) as perhaps they do. Eagles
bring in green bouquets to their mates; dead wood would
build up the nest easier; their renewals help lower the barriers
between our kinds. But a hen hen harrier ('71) took away
a resinous stick I'd brought before she started to lay
and carried it far, on her relief-from-sitting (you saw
her drop it just where she was to leave the tell-tale eggshells
where she'd pick up peat-black water-voles) the white-sand beck shore!

I have watched lammergeier paint himself with ochre
at such a spring as this, far away and since those moorland days
and only later seen wading-birds so stained) back home
– from dibbling for what in this ooze until their smart greys
and golds and warm browns and clean whites) grown old and murky
reddened as ruffs) or godwits' until the moult or they fray
– could this be deliberate) perhaps betraying the brain of a joker?

at an iron chalybeate, spring, Blackamore
for Harry Thompson

129

§

Celebrate with us the hills' standing up
curvetting as curlews calling, vetting
our approach; a thousand displaying dihedrals
and only one of them a harrier's, you are betting
you will eventually decide which music intervals
are appropriate, but we are not listening (Jupp,
Simms, Hewitson, all game-minded, are getting
something else out of the generous occasion.

Harrier in a scarce scatter the whole fells over
we find the cathedral of high-bracken spandrels
fronds green from gold now the scent of clover
below bespeaks 'summer'. This is late nest, candles
are on the chestnuts and we missed the birds displaying
so while we searched Cheviot these were laying…
The hen-bird comes-on to air-rock-wing-buffet
and the child tumbles of shock "like little Miss Muffet"
Undignified to collapse with laughing near such a bird?
but the whole of humankind then seems quite absurd…

Harbottle; to Terry and April and Judith Owston

§

Clever wing-buffets, swinging closed talons
she boxes the bog owl softly, as a bonxie
and quietly, ghostly long wings of the earth
of repeated behaviour; a formula non-violent
and no injury resulting, but a resolution of sorts
each bird going its own way carefully afterward,
whether seriously indeed, or merely at play
they had clashed and would not again many a long day,
easy to say 'territory' – the nests of either *miles* away!

Harriers to roost, on the 'Medicine Line'

doubts in evening shades deliver drabbest of narrow shadows
fenceposts don't cluster, move so, shuffle, play 'tag' game or 'please follow'
faces flatten like owls', muster like a coven, stalk dance-steps slow
out of the prairie fields north and south surely, for quite a distance
frost coming-on, snow so far absent, a front can hardly advance
as at my home border often, air-masses hold moods each in trance
yet few think of even our spirits, the Great Spirit to teach
here or anywhere else, few listen, as these birds seem to reach
upwards with one ear as much as one eye and I want to breach
silence and absence of anything men expect if any wait
like this. But not with nothing in mind we can turn, turning late
because of such unexpected assembly; expect a changed state...

On the 49th parallel, again, 1975 winter.

§

These hours of brightness polishing snowfield so she learns
iceblink binocular as I slowly can adjust burns
retina to control perceptions until sight discerns
under and over glare, I've no nictitating membrane, my stare
must compensate for mirage and deceit distracting nodding ferns
sunset brightness earns hues; the ringtail's taffeta turns
in this light toward red, red to yellow on the frond upturns

Her brood-patch has melted, wet, the lichen on her stone
and she's waddled to another on this blockfield, hasn't flown
– these look-outs after less than an hour are as dry as bone.
Only where she's left a casting are these little tors not alone;
not the less empty for her presence, and she *is* a passing show...
nor, until spring, anything but daw, raven, or crow
and these do not scavenge her leavings; myself and a *wren* do so!

Crossfell, 2008/9

Harrier. Theatre-Prompter

– for shepherd, brother-in-law Howard

who knew, and knows the harriers of Wanney
"nae bother" is all the glad traffic of lambing
– "in peewits' blether gled's music sae canny
only Colin can hear it! an' the morse and the ranny
through the crags are whisslin' and the wind slammin'"
so he took his prompting for verse and for the crack
we've come to hear in *The Gun*. Its quiet at the back
Heather and Cheryl Hogg ensure, and Shitty Rigg –
as if the salvoes still come over his unarmoured deck –
called "Steady"! Slessor and Anderson, pints at the ready,
missing only the likes of Jackie Broon and Billy Pigg…

But the 'poyets' are here, breaking the silence kept
at the harrier's nest where their chicks in full sun slept
though grouse cowered at the spectres overhead
where the gled towered ower careless snipe and 'creep' *
and Baz and Colin were trying to notate the leap
and sweep of winnowing wing on what the breezes said
undisturbed by the long fluting of gawdie**, curlew
for from such rousing chorus in that night we took our cue
and none of us 'finished' the poem or tune, or wanted to.

Wanney Hills, Ridsdale 1983, 1987
* *'moss-creep' - meadow pipit*
** *'gawdie' - golden plover*

Off the Sound of Harris

Soundless where only sea, wind, and bird are heard
groundless swept light as his feathers, father bird
as blue in Hebridean light on machair
as its slacks swales and swathes of milkwort or
as patches of light-blue between milk-clouds there;
these, all, what the eyes of the brains are for
but we couldn't see as far as the Forest shore.

1954, 2005

§

Somewhere within the span, amoebic,
twenty miles of Dumfries well into the season
come-upon her blunt chisel face as in lace
– fronds of the place – eyes coals-bright
fringe of a girl's frock or shawl, light behind
ferns, flourished as wing-feathers on the wind
forever until found, asphodel flowers a few feet
from her ground, coil spring stiff on her mound

my fear from fern flourish feathers forever
where Kenneth had been flayed, face opened,
("buried it for relief in moss green as carrageen")
– sphagnum remembered, best for an open wound…
flushed my face as she grew tall on the nest,
hers, divided my quest between soul and science.

(Dumfries & Galloway) 1974
I had a Home Office permit to approach such a nest.

§

hill cattle ship their terracettes in the dark
breathe heavy, nearing my bivouac in Old Park
whose deer would not have stumbled, woken me up
by their heeding and feeding. Another flask to sup
and I'd have missed the brown gled off her brown bed
away with the others, wanting short-day's-hunt instead
of the long night's vigil. Some of them don't sleep
and fly the day through, rhythm and discipline to keep
me on their by-ways, these ridgeways, looking sideways…
old smell of the beasts heats the cold runnels. A warning
moor-cock challenges, the hill-man's , "Ah'll gie ye wrassel"
across the fell, as across the mart-ring that morning
Jousting tournaments are turning arguments round, all around,
Thus mind wanders here into words over, and overheard
and the eye misses the only pipit that has stirred
so far. Unhurried the harrier behind me, and the bird
has met bird without fuss, transaction without hassle
in her stride of air, but has taken her prey to her ground

§

Bolam Howie doesn't kna
(he cracks in the pub the neet)
he's got big ha'ks on his fell
it wants dykin up theer, ye ken.
He's gotten Boot Farm, and then
a gardin the grass's higher in than.
In looking at you, if he's to tell
me, who kna's em, *he* dinna kna weel
sound-as-a-pound herd's the only way
he can be, you can be sure of him
because of his care, his will on the hill
itsel' over the generations of his livin'
an' as weel as him ye can trust the wife
as she *feels* the ha'ks flee the winn.

22.11.84

§

en echelon with himself before
ever she appears on her horn-
of-advance-and-turning-the-corner;
sickles of impi, buffalo or
gleaming welds each their lightning gather:
two hawk-shapes now tower together
– she inverts for the 'food-pass' hover...

patient, persistent as waving corn
circling *circus* is waiting his turn
to bring him round with no fuss to her,
touch-talons at transfer. Harvest born.

Harish 1959

§

alarming loud, as a harrier came over the hay
partridge hurried out, hardly in the air, I'd say
brushing the stubble. But both talons closed neat
catch, fingers underneath, at a best fielder's feet:
not lingering, gled ghosted gliding away:
though I was behind the dyke there in his way
his right to Stainmore's best gamemeat-and-sweet!

Co. Durham 1955, 2005

§

The blue-hawk which, in the Tyne Gap
dropped in front of us from his clear blue sky
(– nervous, or tribute, and as if doffing his cap?)
that cast-lamb's genitals you and I
supposed must have been meant for young in the nest
unless scavenged and then discarded as useless…
Twenty years on found one as a nest-ornament…

North Pennines 1970, 2006. Compare the 1986 incident (p.36)

For an opener-up; a Priorsdale Harrier

She's instituting control thus by beating her bounds
Selling streamers, tattered ribbons of those gulls
summer blackheadeds who patrol harrier grounds
as if by prior arrangement a lord declares to his fools
– condensed from our overview their scatters constitute crowds –

I've not seen a harrier strike at a rocketting grouse
as I have the peregrine, and eagle – once in Easter Ross
though the harrier is their challenger over this heather
and takes their chicks and half-grown young she comes across.
This is the smallest fraction of what passes or comes together
and I have to try the picture whilst under its skies
and while I have its light of the moment in my eyes
which comes to some who assume or require instant report, fine or dross,
impatient not only from passion – and so my attempted work must surprise...

Priorsdale, 1969

§

The challenge of flying the length of Souter Fell
in this south wind has March bumblebees humming
of wing-mechanism, off the marchgrasses lifting a rhythm
onto air as clear as you can now see her coming
snipe and pipits' descents, notwithstanding their thrumming
are tied in the ringtails' progress, beat of her silent drumming.
Gills gutters utterly siller under this swelling light
Swinging the blue-hawk her mate the other pendulum of the fell.
Overhead gulls and raven manage the challenge quite well...

for Peter Robinson, 1971

Life careless of convenience

shows only when we are ready for comfort
dragging our feet up through the stiff heather;
he comes into our lank crop, a sickle
cutting our cares as burning and swithens
intimate to the ground as a prayeer on prairie
scythe handled by a champion in rushesedge
gilt of the morning on his trailing-edge
dark band of pigment as of the dew's wetness
yet lit silver and gold of grass-pollen
powdered and perfumed dandy of grazing
glazing, pale, adhesive: a culture
shines on our reflection passive, pastoral
sweeps crescent shape sheer 'blue-hawk'.

Collin Fell 1978

§

curlew's less-usual bubbling; *tremolo*
warning to the young, running; below,
who cannot fly yet, knows the Spirit of the Common
as John Clare did – and its distinction
from moor and fen, tundra and rough pasture
(and seemed to prefer its ambience to any other)
and as this harrier does, if not all harriers,
having learned how to find prey upon its face
as we once also watched lesser but similar grace
disport over these upland acres a whole family
of eight ling owls 'rationally, rhythmically'; "see
how they cover, quarter the ground closely, each
keeping its fellow within a watching-reach;
imitation for education is no barrier"!

(for Sir Mark Allen)
Blackburn Common and The Dargues Hope
Northumberland

Ringtail Harrier at Otterburn Training Area

with the gaining dawn direction succession
strengthening from the sunrise colour after
colour strengthens lengthens laid-on impression
on impression surely for her eyes as for mine
less surely for the minds, or for her mind
expecting her superior perception
millennia on millennia a hunter
condensed into a few years' education
for a few more years life-expectation
in fullness of fine form and plumage
single-purpose as we might wrongly suppose;
no loneliness whatever our perception;
no organism exists in isolation. Damage
only enlightenment when any such sun rose.
At last lights on crest of Viking tumulus
as on his helm or shield again flashing
gleam off its wet bleeberry eyes under lashing –
the rain then in the way things are remembered
rightly is often the wrong way round for our tropes
transforming perceptions as passing in this cumulus
as transient as the light, yet still as full of hopes

RA 1388

From His Home, with Old Alan (Watson)

The showy goosander, from his home far at Fair View
lances the alders along the river, never near them,
misses the spear of the heron, lifts into the blue
the buzzard; too dignified to protest – squawk,
intrigues deer where we once watched dark Marsh Harrier
rattles dry old Northern Dock, many another stem
of the Melancholy Thistle, puts up at last Blue Hawk…

Overhead but not heard by anyone here below
save me, the gabbling, old Alan's head on his pillow
within walls which do not contain him, empty window,
high geese change flight-leader, say what they know as they go…
one of those gatherings for which he yet remains shepherd
long past retirement still of his real employment.
they say – 'oh, the molecatcher'; but have any heard
the learned depth of his crack of all we do not know?
His deportment largely unvisited, important…

The harrier soars, behind and below the buzzard
(often here there are four or more species of raptors –
their 'rare raptors' – in the air at once – at no great hazard
to one another; but there won't be room for the Kite
if the others are to thrive, continue to recover
this morning after thoughtless persecution's long night…
such persecution still affects the hen-harrier.

§

– "about as much stuffing as an empty potato-sack
flapping on the wind; couldn't pull the skin back
on one of granny's rice puddings," yet about that time
Kenneth Richmond, near a nest, was surprised by attack
after attack from a ringtail in these Southern Uplands
and we, many years later, were dissuaded of a climb
on crags beside a nest-site in Middle Border haughlands
we didn't know was there, by aggressions firmly pressed-home
and missed, illusory, 'safety' of the (cardboard) "bone-dome"

*(bone-dome: Thetford Industries pressed-pulp lightweight
miners' helmet used for caving and climbing also)*

*in mem. W. K. Richmond.
Dumfries and Galloway*

§

The evening-class-weekend-excursion looks around
and three or four (not the retired forester, and not
the young farmer, or the veteran gamekeeper)
Declared at once for "barren-ness", lack-of-life…
I asked what would indicate life – say a lot
of noise? No bird sang in that "dismal" season? –
not even a grouse showed from that dark ground
which struck the 'keeper as "a bit peculiar"
on such a good moor; but he'd see the reason…

"What about rhythm?" I asked the young wife
of the young farmer, didn't expect to get an answer;
"Let's inspect the miles out and across the horizon"
After a few minutes only the distant bounce got
through to everyone; the beat, beating of harrier…

1968

§

Garrigill 2010 3rd April c. 11 a.m.

As seen from my living-room window
a blue-hawk crosses the Gatehead end
of the village. I was waiting for Tom
in a lull of the rain. The peregrine
Rex and I had been watching had gone
though fieldfare flocks fill the meadow
(Nattrass's) until their harsh calls blend.

Then suddenly stopped, and the hundreds lifted
as one. And had the falcon returned?
Even outside I could see 'nothing'
further, though the peewits and curlews had shifted
up the fell to judge from their voices fading
and something at the back of my neck burned

A few hours later I recovered under
this currick's little lee-side overhang
a poor ploat – most feathers had blown
whilst they still were dry but there sang
the foot and booted tarsus of one
of the sub-family of the true thrushes:
this currick climbed – to the nearest outcrop
harriers repair to on their rare
visits so close to the settlement; to stop
and watch from. As do merlins there
and bog owls. I watched the sudden rushes
of returning fieldfares against the rains hissing
in the sivs and couldn't tell there was one missing…

§

To watch the same hen-harrier on successive days would have been remarkable some years ago; but these birds have been doing well, at least in Scotland, and on our high fells are not now an unexpected sight. Their characteristic slow hunting and fine aerobatics are great attributes. A fellow watcher from an adjacent dale *was* unexpected, though I've met him before. These encounters were fortuitous…

As I arrived the bird had flushed a party of sixteen golden plover and was pursuing them in the manner expected more of a *merlin*; low fast zigzagging, using the ripples of the land to tack. All their speeds were reduced by a stiff westerly they were flying into down dale; why had the plovers elected to fly into such a wind and why didn't they go to ground in the tussocks, rushes or borrans about? I have seen hunted birds hide in the cover of old walls; here there was neither bracken, rank heather nor whins and the pursuit was in the open over a mile and a half at least before the harrier landed on a ruin of a dyke sheltered by spoil to the windward but still giving good vantage, where she faced away from me and sank onto her long tarsi in an evidently resting position she was to hold for half-an-hour.

The pursued plover flock had spread rather than bunched – I thought the harrier's rushes from one side to the other had been to pick out or pick up a laggard or slower bird; but it had looked more like shepherding them along as they bunched each time her 'energy wasting' approaches closed on one or more outriders. None had been approached closer than, say, fifteen feet and all had twisted and turned only on those approaches of the big predator, as if they had eyes in the back of their heads.

We had not wanted to interfere, but we followed-up the plover flock at a distance and into the view of the harrier, which had surely already seen us when the chase started, and was well aware of the onlookers. It is my rule not to get in the way, even if it means missing a 'kill' or some other observation. Clearly now the harrier was resting, alert but weary. My fellow watcher had been studying her quartering for some time before she raised the plover flock; she'd made scores of low sweeps across the fell to the eastward, alternately low and at moderate height working into the wind. Steadily, hovering and turning with the wind from time to time. I have watched what I take to be the same bird, with distinctive markings indicating her youth, on several occasions in recent weeks. She has managed to catch a range of prey, mainly birds in hard weather and rabbits; and such as would not upset a cautious gamekeeper…

Hen Harriers Displaying

Sky now where nothing else can be found
nor sound for a far lark's hesitant rhyming.
They are both Up! overseeing bounds
high-pastures slanted to sun's climbing
(blinding the black-cock straining to see)
for these are their best hunting-grounds
vole-coursed street, metropolises
with moss-creepers, whaups, pewits, gawdies.
Sheer overlooking High, Middle, Low Lee,
harriers pair over swidden, mounds, swalleys
their dead-ground for maybe nest-to-be…

Smaller seems to have the greater power
or motive – his is the steepling tower
yellow bangles hang, dihedral angle
with some package, blackish. Her brown dangle
rocks from the perpendicular fathoms below
a dance of swinging and sashaying so slow
sun she interrupts has time to warm us…
strong in late April. We almost miss the move
flipped on to her back, talons toward him to prove
the aim of his bomb-run effortless, precise
of their bond, our example, this the device!

[moss-creepers: meadow pipits;
whaups: curlews;
peewits: lapwings;
gaudies: golden plovers.
The gift-package was a mole]

1958, 1967, 1979.

§

Herringshoal skies over from the coast
'do not write in the newspaper what you love the most'
hush off the floods sufficiently eloquent
ominous ever before our eyes opened at the "ghost" –
which hawk had stood un-noticed upon a post
at her elbow, Sun rising, she, expectant,
for she knew them, these her water-meadows.

Their most silent presence, grey as 'errn' *
threw across between us strengthening shadow of the cross
the way a cormorant had at the Farne
but was not drying his wings, for I was to learn
stretching in preen, essential maintenance
flying machine as if of doped paper, wire
nerve-net as tense as us for action.

Flooded ings great mirrors for acres
with the wind still. "We need this, and else very little"
Derwentland farmer's daughter 'taught by nature'
ablaze at the eyes from the water and the skies, attends
blue hawk, as another had, Black Hawk Island
"without being able to *say* very much about it" then
but not surprised as I was not surprised at her

singing within as if the curlews had come early
before the threat of 'development' to that whole river system
came a few years' later, deemed inefficient
waste when water gets scarce, and ripe for 'recreation'
waterfowl to go as the wildfowlers were gone
she could work in a supermarket in the distant town
her 'green thoughts in a green shade' turn sour to brown.

* *heron*

145

A First Harrier

Until we lived the water, river, beck and sike
pond, estuary, bog-peaty-pools
rightly she ranked us gowks, fools
overlooking sense and truth until we stumbled
on the spell, stilled every reed in the marsh.

about, surely, her deliberate business
doesn't need to be so silent, either –
when she *does* speak she can be squeaking, or harsh
like every frog in the beck head's claggy flush
unmoving until she has slowly flown-over

left us a silence, my sister amazed
our dialect aunties's eyes getting glazed
this 'first', not only of uplands deployment
but ranging as we were the Cleveland embayment
bottomland sheltered under the escarpment.

§

Rhythmic as the surges through seedheads, if not as deep,
golden wheat, barley, silver and gold the wide wings sweep,
with the Barn Owls – also silver and gold seen in some light.
Harriers work with the wind to see, if they have the angle right
and the speed, to the base of the palisades where shelter's the least
as Ronald showed us for a Pallid harrier of the east –
and the Hen Harrier is now with us less over cultivation
than the Montagu's his cousin – close enough for confusion
of identity. Their urges resonant with the winds' searching
merge defined species as one way of life beyond our reaching
for definition, as this description proves inadequate depiction!

§

not from the highest soaring of the raven
does he dispose, not from hovering kestrel;
less dependent on winds up the escarpment,
sees under skirts of fell fogs' low firmament.
not from the great height either of the eagle
does he roll out the dales and vales as easy,
teases-out waves of land as made off the sea:
strand-flats, machair, dune fields, terraced raised-beaches,
reach by reach so comprehending the rivers
restores our grasp of landscape, all the wonders
own map – interpreter contour by contour...

is a hypnotic power filling the sail in us hard
something the shortear owl shares, not kestrel or buzzard
unfading, unfailing wake that carries us so along
seasurge carefree imitating all advancing sea-song
roll of all watters, this lake. Receding, wave insists on
irrational irritation as at smudged horizon;
a blow to the solar plexus which nothing else explains
until that realisation with onset of the rains! –
that unexpected hawkish presence, that uneasiness
come on for no other reason we can guess

Bassenthwaite 1986

§

silent music of the transecting's movement
the one thing not lost on the moor's wind
white ring at her tail wringing some dilute pigment
she 'sings' from it and wing edge and her ruff
an Elizabethan dancer, doublet of bedewed stuff
and fritillary-markings streaks are spinned
slashed-sleeves breadth of wing and bastard-wing
emphasising gesture the grain of land suggested

and so over other counties and continents
patterns set for the joys of appreciation
in increase of awareness and of recognition
already there under another name – "nudem nomen"
as the opener-up of landscape went with us
everywhere the bird, surely long of good omen
as the moors represent home, her elegant movement
their majesty, a modesty. Great sweeps of range
for her, for us. Two days, above Egton Grange…

§

New snow showed, four feet apart,
fine 'finger' prints to the left, to the right,
feather-formula correct for the species
precise as the blood spots at their heart.
The only time I had this bird 'in sight'
that day. A few feet ahead fresh rabbit faeces
in more spots of blood not needing analysis…

§

memo to Robert MacFarlane (Guardian 26.09.09)

I'm sure you are sincere in behind
'environment' reviews for which you're waged
in a rather fashionable newspaper
but this is what has some enraged:
decades of 'nature' just to much of us wallpaper
on behalf of harriers, for example,
hearts and minds have not been engaged
emotion is rationed-out to a sample…

You'll look long before you find a hind
or a 'keeper to really take care
to do other than he's told, and blind…
even 'twitchers' often show 'the ignorant stare':
there was a time when merlins' eggs were
stamped on the same way just over there…

§

It may be a long long way away
but the eye fills with this bird of prey
grey, so easy to suggest is laconic.
Whatever ground or weather he flies on
part of the scene, not passing, tectonic
as last week's bursting of his bog
time as transformed by his varying beat
of wing and of route in cold or heat.

Where merlin and sterling peregrine
finding nothing here to their liking
raise a pursuit of place itself, spin
away in deliberate grace, more Viking
restlessness perhaps, and of that kin
his patient persistence is striking…

Ringtail Harrier

Comes to the same rippled shadows
that she left at this hour yesterday
on these same falling-river shallows
– some are her own, and some the grey .
of these alders' never the same twice as she knows
nor is she; so her approach varies, her going-away

coming off the hill she has caught a pipit
light, loose in her foot she has brought with it
(her nest and her young two miles behind her)
a need to watch flood-water or listen, the tones
and melody wandering over lichened stones
like us itching midges does music remind her
of time, its ritual? Not putting the pipit down to wash
where the knuckles and froth invite, Hadyad Wath
hovers back and forth under alders' arches untouched
you agree the controlled sway-dance of her standard verse
which works over the fell and the bog haggs she's hushed.*
And she's away the way she has come, precise in reverse.

(1982)
* *pun intended, she's silenced these bird walks and revealed them as the miners'*
'hushing' has – her patrols in a sense remove the superficial, show the structure
and, here and there, the 'productive' vein…

§

learning from him to use the contours
to hide myself, down on an elbow
crouching, crouch-climbing-scrambling lures
alarms, tell-tale shadow on the snow…

§

Beyond a Desert Lark, sounding strangely loud
this theatre lightens far, pietist sigh,
keeps heaped-up as towers of immature cloud
sky, sleeping over top-gallants, unlikely, high.
Curtains lift the middle-distance, ever slow
tilt perspective with, approach rear sky
widening horizons' perpetual snow.

Foothills enlarge their measure at a canter
folds drape to our feet, merge slowly serge to sage
and lift the censer, back-and-forth quarterer
cultivator of 'mice' below its Ice Age
meadows and high grasslands – old 'marsh'-harrier
cadence within all our histories engage
in the constant, signed by this gene-carrier.

Central Asia 1986

§

Co. Durham, May 28, 2002.

Despite distance, size, light, this morning
is this a crane flying, high; a floating raft
(steady as a heron over the Greta's colder awning)
toward Skerne, turning on its axis as a cardan-shaft
(but may be careless of rivers' courses, anyway
wanting carrlands reed feathered garlands)

                *

Tees offers, teases, opening-up further space
but Yarm and Eaglescliff pass under this bird's pace
playing a riff sparkling light, floods below
yet going out of right, soon outruns own shadow
and we, even more slow, have nowhere to go…

Blue Hawk Hunting

(To Basil Bunting)

looking after his progress landscape zones into light
distant or near, hazy or clear, dark'ning or bright
dissolving is not regress, even for your "poor old eyes"
there registers, resistless as ever, delight; "Surprise"!

the only time I've watched a blue-hawk from my garden
there; and he's ringed the Dunterley to Gorcock horizon
(even when Mark Allen was here for seven raptors
– the harrier a ringtail, merlin, kestrel, spar, buzzard, goshawk, peregrine)
and, for all three of us, these watchings and these seeings
strongly increase our sense, awareness of the well-formedß being…

as observations can become art by love
and not by contrivance, and science can come
by craftsmanship, let's try for both, hand-in-glove
against the cold coming yet; "yes, you'll forget death":
beside the wood-in-trouble-you can get breath
– and a "lungful of this helps us take-on the rhythm"
as wide long beech-boughs dip in recognition
of wind never the same two days – "yes an animation"
by analogy, with that motion wind-winged bird takes
(D'Arcy Thompson rightly a principle)… makes
his prey in this shelter a – breathless Stock Dove.

Woodhead, Tarset with Bunting
in an autumn gale, 1983,
'showing him' a Blue-Hawk

From the harriers' roost, again the dispersal

Four of the seven ungathering, low, together;
first sign of them at strengthening first light a grouse pack
packing behind as red-badged redpolls and lintwhites fled
as something this weird Borders air went wet and slack
and en echelon these sisters silently spread the fell;
three falling on three grouse families in still heather.
recall how harrowing* arrows on that Halidon Hill
cut down bonneted Scots chiltrons to their last feather

As they are all part of the undercurrent of the wind,
these prey species for the hunters who rode the wind better
set its perspectives in the mind of those watchers, 'eyes skinned',
who read the signs as the hunters themselves, to the letter...

Cheviots Borders, June 1978

* 'harrowing', *a term used for the tactic of deploying (English) archers not in line
but in vees, and shooting from each limb of the vee at the 'hedgehog' rounded
defensive formation of the Scots on either side as well as those in front. Here, a 'vee'
of four harriers.*

Fellside in November Sun

Watching the flies dance vertically
over sivs, tussocks, and thistles, did he
remember his own sky-diving those spring days
hill-mist mate below in excited haze?
– joyous all these dancers seem to me to be
eye-sharpening after passion, or me
surprised at his now clouding-over sight
(and if you think I 'anthropomorphise',
yes he's following movements, moving head and eyes
in universal sun-given rhythm). Rapt I crept *in front*
then backed away again, feeling I had no right…

§

Mobbed at times by all and the smallest birds around;
'hookbill' bullied by buzzards and falcons, I've found
seeming meek, the harrier on its own ground
will attack other open-fell birds-of-prey
especially those owls which hunt there by day;
in this region there are several such species
(yet only one breeds there under their aegis) –
the short-eared owl, often mistaken at a distance
for the harrier; a slow day-flier, at a glance
so similar – and so unexpected here for an owl
fell men often call "bog owl" or "ling owl".
Much more rarely here the woodlands' long-eared owl
will fly the moors in daylight and twilight
and so will the little-owl – a hunter so slight
but intent on the insect-crop on these hills;
the bigger birds also often resort to these lesser kills
but hardly ever the familiar, ghostly barn owl
– and some fellsides know the ubiquitous tawny-owl…

'The Hellum'

Blasts of the Helmwind "turn grass blue"
the blue of glass under a blue sky
the way I've seen catabatics in the Rockies do
when hardly a bird has been able to fly
but one which will, who needs to be on the wing
and may take that red winged blackie cowering
is the blue of tested metal, and mettle true…

§

On Ronnie's farm, fell fields favoured by fieldfares
flocked also droves of roving
Peewit Green and Golden Plover
a few, very few of forty odd thousands over the years
of each of these species proved something different
just as a few days, very few, brought the harriers
over the long winters there where I went
with each bird counting, no matter what seen or heard
followed through daylight alert every herd

Fairly the harrier rove found out the ill favoured few
fair blew in its wind such occasional feather-strew
as I picked out once a blackthroated thrush in the rush
rushes and numbers through I stumbled to flush,
flushes of the hill sills and bums hid at night the ground
signatures of fox scentless signal-head sentinels sensed, found
fled herds through my sleeplessness away to another
favoured if far-flung face on another's farm
plover-place flocks offered harbour from harm

East High Ridge and beyond from Greystead and Wasdhead
1983-92

Tinctures (in the heraldic sense)

Colours on the hill blaze never yet the same
light, air varying with more than time and sun
wind's and season's hollow ways (though they repeat)
to find our feet so we can find the strays
climbing limit of vision; rising horizon.
consider the blue that is on or off snow
glows the pink and red of sunrise and sunset
is to do with the clear blue sky overhead
also with the tones of the 'blue hawk', I said.

§

over the broad moors the haze often merges the birds
with waving heather mirage in its own roll of wave
obscures grasses. Not approaching where the nest might be
if we have deduced it correctly. First is their privacy,
there will be a sufficiently distant place to watch from.
occupied nests bring out the dramatic, and the brave
aggression of the harriers – beyond my feeble words...!

how often the plucking-sites scatter the base home range
harriers need, have to leave evidence in open view
despite their own ability often to de-'materialise'.
Their presence, as ours, is given away by the spies
especially the crows, the peewit, and the curlews
whose sharp alarm calls "tyweeyu", "twyoo"
and the grouse shout out with their bad grace...

Dihedral

a figure in the skies of much of the world
especially the world of open skies over open ground
from wide upland plateaux to coastal marshes
and including the great plains, the lesser basins
the sod-turned former prairie breadbaskets and cornbelts
rice fields and forest-edges, bogs and (grouse)-moors
a figure to emphasise also hovering kestrel

a figure stationary to the drive-by 'analysis',
or moving stately and steadily as if to measure us
against the land by the harrier's own yardstick,
vision better than ours, hearing better than ours
purpose, life-attitude, economy so foreign to us
to be brought down often early by a single barrel shot
as having overflown or threatened our interests…

one rode the dipslope of my youth's home escarpment
angled to wind and his own persistent waveform
storms cannot breakdown his aerodynamic uplift
light wing load ironies skyline crucifixion or gibbet.
On this occasion over unthreatened spring dotterel
we had come to see, to be faced by the mystery
which shouldn't be, crossing presumption of tragedy…

for Athol Wallis and Gordon 1968, rev. 2008

(Signs of Early Autumn, Tynedale)

Up the fell as, and after, the shooters' roll down
"sixty-eight brace" (off thousands of acres) to be entered.
What emotion the falcon off their beats, of bloodied crown
from fluent bill-strike, she in the neck of that one grouse?

Settles at roost with usual unmistakable frown,
face as clean as a whistle. Hunting the disoriented
has been easy for her, though she's of smaller species
than peregrine; she has compensatory *spirit* in
like that even smaller hunter of this fell, a merlin,
and, like Hobie Noble is banished off her 'own country'
outlaw to fly into England 'to take her prey'
for she is hobby and noble as any ballads say!

I'm singing these ballads of Noble, The Side, and The Hay
and Archie of Cawfield and Percy Reed's last Rederdale day,
when a flock of one-forty-nine very dark redwings just
pitches in, calling weakly each other, well short of dusk
– so new the harrier later overflies them, *his* route to roost
routine already, for they're in the 'dead ground' of hushes.
He's slower to react, but most are hidden in rushes
and there's no more killing time, and it's at the sun's last ray…

August 28ᵗʰ 2007

§

Often across Shap's high limestone pastures, by A6
and the minor roads, since the days of the 'road burners'
The Northern Roadburners' rides exploring, Jungle Caff coffee
pheasant and partridge and lagomorphs "nice little earners";
often across Stainmore, Ribblehead, the 'fifties and 'sixties
and of course, as now, fringes of their rough-grazing hills
Bollands and Howgills, I'd like to stop to admire "Ringtills"
and "Blue-ees" beating against the wind on their special ease
as at high sky-spirals and dives over the mate and the nest
stopping often to 'follow'. Eddie Flintoff, find the nest
'unlicensed', untold discoveries where some birders only guessed...

Near Staveley a Hobby sweeps away the tops of the trees
steering over Harter not far away the Golden Eagle
from a great height inspects both the wind-sides and lees
of mountainsides below, few adjustments and regal
Barrie and I, and Peter and I, riding in-between
with the swallow around our heads for the turbulence
and other insects in the slipstream of each machine
prefer, mutual attention honourable, a gled
from somewhere about High Arse, proceeds ahead
same way I've known harriers preceding, or succeeding,
or at point; curious, or for prey flushed up, – their commonsense.

Westmorland, 1964, 1994

§

...grasses lying dead, flying bents on the wind
spin on their axis, spikelets and each rachis
with dust off the dried peat of our erosion
red cottongrass debris contributes to frass
where Obtrush Ruck raises its own dead head
carrier wind deposits seeds in store
for the snow-bunting to come, the starling now
and the harrier sails on alone, lone prow
cutting airway over Aira and Holcus
as steady an average wind prairie raises
and the tundras, in their seasonal praises...

Blackamore, 1959
[Obtrush Ruck: a cairn considered ancient]

§

...this is the centenary of Tunguska
just one minor event in earth-history
few billion years this planet has lasted
(they explained to me flying over, nineteen-eighty
  "biggest thing in the known history of Russia
    with hundreds of millions of trees blasted")
  Conifer statistics are understated
people hundreds of square miles devastated
was only a comet's ice-nose the carrier
down below the familiar rhythm, reviver
repeats, ubiquitous ringtail harrier...

2007 (Siberia, 1980)

§

...in the dissected castings surprised to find
a part-digested mennin*, scores of its scales
more than once in springtime, which brings to mind
harrier flights low over becks, sikes and swales
floods and spates, flood-debris and the back-ponding
where I've seen them go for frogs and water-voles.
I use the dialect word* here, respecting and responding
to those Borderers and shepherds who have told
me of these birds, and owls, fishing the merse,
across the mosses and Solway and Border mires
seen to lift eels – "strips of inner tubes of tyres"!

Cheviots, late 1960s
[mennin: minnow]

§

The cadence of a Strathspey, played slow
yet with its opening bars' urgency
she took off and started quartering into the blow
and buffeting the 'winds o' Kielder's' sashay

They say the Tynedale fells for miles
seem 'nowt but nothingness'
whilst all the whiles
round and round flee these indigenes
regular over the same bit o' ground
even after they *must* have found
summat ti eat for the nest!

For such a bird all the dales are one
every common and fellside could be available
but too many of their 'smitt -spots' are gone...

For Bill Lancaster of Blaydon and Haydon Bridge
his Northern Review *promoting Northern sense and letters*

Sundaysight

theirs not the image of 'the noble falcon'
harriers are somehow passed-over
(good for them) by the image-makers
and they are not made to hunt for us
merely some kind of bleak ground rover
(nests, as here, regularly trodden underfoot
in the interests of *gamebirds* or midden-rakers)
and, mistaken for the Tarset's one sparrowhawk,
stalked by some ignorant shotgun carriers.
Pipits seized on their ladders by harriers
(exultant in their switchback display flights
which bring emotion to dingdoon barriers)
are their regular prey. Give them their rights.

§

Closeness, of itself, of to what this is over and over
is in a harrier's concentration over all its known earth
low-flying gives perspectives for the quarry waders;
he's had loose chicks, peewit and redshank, off the verge
and tarmac itself, vulnerable himself by coming – by
and coming – by culling, trimming the moon now June
reduces on her part piping – epiphanies of oystercatchers

fractals wavy BlackBurn encounter every delta
tracking triangles fractured toe-prints maybe to catch
dainty May's so-called Common Sandpiper off-guard
as on my Dargues Hope study-area nearby, where hard
practise confirms less sandpipers now know less harriers,
As Charles Lyell misled Charles Darwin, we change the world
negatively, for the worse always, don't adapt to her.

For David McCracken 1990, 1999

§

She floats out of the spruce sticks – her pinions
dip swirlsquaresshimmerscale-skin liquid
as she passes over caressing to put up snipe
the old meadows of Bradburn, now as extinct
as its buildings and people except old Tom
surviving to tell the tale to me, Alston.
You breathe on the glass, take a soft cloth to wipe

– at Catless her cutlass swung
the once to fell, picked up in one swoop
and for two miles headfirst hung
blackcock tight back in the coop
cuddled in her long legs and talons
rising and falling ride, the great wings
needing deeper beats, head-nodding swings

– over the lank grasses making for haytime
toward Willowbog she rows as heavily
carrying huge seed herself – who could foresee
the blackgame to extinction through forestry?

1959, 1999

For Tom and Kathryn

§

Her own eggs, their ham, her mother's fresh bread
white as her liberty, more than a picnic spread
(went something of the music of a Charles Wesley hymn
"the boy will go with you; you go with him"
her hill farmer father had impressed on her,
"enjoy the day; we make our own weather")

*

After, she clutches her breeze-cooled hands together
spreading newly-relaxed in the winter heather
– those moments eyes sharpen with a vision –
and declares for the perfect loving occasion's
grand setting though "cosy as the hare in its form"
"so pastoral" though the fells will brew up a storm.

*

The bird only a moment forgotten for the warm
the pastoral is for us the form
assumed here by erotic thought…
Rise and fall which the harrier brought
for our supine watching sky-diving display
hour after hour along a long day

Harriers at a winter roost; a North Dakota marsh

When they first come in, some of them
play the fool, a little, like children
home from school, sure spirit of kindred.
They bring in bits of the world they've travelled to
(old-timers' words in the township bar still do)
consonant to the mist in the marsh, a few
disappear from sight right away, so stationary.

Morning they disperse in order reverse of assembly
those further in later to light's warning reveille
signals between them, of gesture, mantling quietly
leaving the roost singly, with the meadow lark on the wing
theirs the dribble of reluctant labourers, they can't sing
perhaps bored with relations and neighbours only standing
wrapped all night in themselves, tedious limb-shifting...

Murmurs in the reedgrass and above it as the conclave
sages grey and scarfed away, the hesitant wave
nervously reasserts on more wind than night gave
no clearer clues needed for my mind's, way's direction
coming up from the earth less and less regeneration
of the song I am late to learn, in communication
from clans to less-closed clans, 'make it new'.*

Ezra Pound, to us all

An Irish Opinion

What, there in the bar, I was meaning to say
was just the bird you call the "hen-harrier"
is the shake of the bag of the birds-of-prey –
you know; mixing some 'shite hawk' and 'fuck-the-gale',
'bohg-owl'* and more, oh, some ghostly stray
from all the cemeteries from Kinsale
to Kerry; it's as much as you'd get today
of an *eagle* in any place in Ireland –
and no matter how much you could pay!

(with Willie Gallagher, West Cork, Eire)

on another occasion he called it boggart-owl;
'bog owl' is also common in north Britain (1958)

§

So many 'blank' patrols, especially in winter,
'fruitless' scouring across miles of bent and heather
yet of course none of these are empty, they show
other details to those who are there to know
accumulatively. Winters started thus in 'forty-seven
(your ride from Fellgate Farm was cancelled out
yet you walked the miles to Corney church, to shout
"where are you husband to be" into the hard blizzard
escorted by a blue hawk, you said, "not even a buzzard"
on Black Combe.) I told the story after her wake
– "now make something reet about it, for her sake"!

For Doris Little, who kept the café on
Front Street (dec.), Alston Moor 1997

§

Your letter despite its words has found me out
who has been feeling, looking for words for this flight;
reckoning chords at one part of the boundary
full of expectations varying with the coast
where the delivery is of the great Gare foghorn
revolving with the moon, repeating with the harrier.

Nothing could be more natural, it seems to us,
at intervals stilling the wading birds, even the gulls
in the lulls the low sweetness of a woman's voice
full of repercussions in the mirk for such a boy
and yet the harrier flutters, seen and unseen, nearer
and nearer, with other obscurities dispersing, returning.

Marley, Blezard, Richmond, Rowan, Holder, all
have learned and pass on, differentially, intervals
for the silent song which one day may not be so quiet
as not to be heard within ribcage and sea-wall
another glow going through all we call 'nature'
the unsayable flight of the nimble harrier.

(with my mother, Teesmouth)

§

Both wee burns' and great rivers' divides
mossy rounded summits, heather grown sides
the Border Hills run, so apt for Boundary Rides,
from the North Sea-side right across to the Irish Sea
ill-drained grasslands and forest for life-history   .
('moss-troopers' once) black grouse and all life primary
as the rocks are; Ordovician and Silurian
highly folded old rocks raised, yet worn of erosion
to sculpted forms and curving lines' expression:
great blocks of similar but seamed rocks, a uniforming
apparent, that nature's living variability hides!

These hills stretch spaces made for the gled and gleds
which ever for me have helped define the long watersheds
now this way turned, now that, at cairn and boulder-beds,
along broad summit ridges, at noops' outcrop edges.
Eastward more distinctive 'laws', yet with wild goat ledges
like the great slag uplands westward, cottongrass and sedges
some of them plugs in the necks of former, cold, volcanoes;
some with their features under masks of blanket bog flows
some carved by facets of glaciation; much fretting shows,
landslips ancient and recent, frost-shatter, ice-wedged,
all over she, the gled, occasional feather secretly sheds.

(The year harriers were away)

Feet find their way there year after year yet
empty hollow but for its rind of charnel
and old down; some presence wisps of the carnal
of dark campsite of a memory might be forever
another season has pressed into the form of a hare
brown fur on lichen and the lank worn heather
where she has left just a trace of her leveret.

This not far from the deserted gypsy encampment
your friend Janice must have lived at, now moved-on
where the harriers tolerated 'because of' the nomads
and by them? Surely not a complete ignorance
did each of you learn to love on that lingy common
the keeper's "between hawk and shitehawk" was meant
to insult you, last-laughing Susan Crompton!...

§

And at one time she's a Slack Kite posed
at another a Marsh Harrier, as majestic;
at yet another an almost-buzzard laconic
almost-soaring on some thermal we've supposed

Certainly not like a kestrel, or any other falcon
appearing less purposive, hardly settled on a line
she spins and quarters, dips and rises gently, fine
flying about her load the lodestone of direction
worked out by observations of the ground – below
closer than mere movement of prey. She will know
the terrain so intimately she'll detect the pipit's shadow.

§

like all her kind, two gold rings she dangles
when her talons close the circles, hanging bangles,
her cere is as old gold, or red with a killing
(blue-horn blown in her youth, – the long up-skilling);
hunting giving a glow also to her tawny ruff,
– courtiers' badge – but not for her the curse of deference –
the more to outwit competitor or prey – her bold bluff
of "owlishness", slowness perhaps, or bafflement's a defence
against recognition of just what she *is*, long enough…

(Diurnal raptorial birds generally have bright-yellow legs and feet)

§

She has the wise delicacy
to carry the empty eggshells away
carefully, and they are often perfect;
perhaps this is to foil the fox
or other 'vermin' away from the nest
– 'hygiene' hardly applies to these birds
living in shambles, bones, beetle-shards…

§

…yet the prairie-states' statebirds
are meadowlarks, not buzzards
not harriers, not even eagles
because their farmers are Teutons
Clearances Scots, not Tetons
or Osages, Chicken-raisers,
sodbreakers, shoot *Hen Harriers*…

Kansas, the Jay Hawk State, 1977

Harriers give way

The moment fell wind draws back toward dawn
she shimmers off, teases, tacks into her track
off the roost after a sprinter's falling – starts
stalling, tempting me to follow, but she can
shoot the bridge, and scorn my many obstacles.

Foolish enough to forget my own strictures
of 'blind' slopes and lines-of-sight, for each
of us. Middleton's keeper had warned me of
"not shuttin' off" this roost of "moor-buzzards"
I lost the lot going-off on their directions.

But I was stopped short at the rigg summit
by 'an eagle of a buzzard' I'd put up, to soar
stately more than the buzzard or my harriers:
a first for me for this dale winter Roughleg
rich buff, handsome white, – "of the snow and hoar"!

(from 1960)

§

When these forests were young they knew more slim harriers,
Several pairs of hen harriers for years, a few Montagu's harriers
thanks to protection for them, ironically, by some foresters
(the blackgame were murdered there by accountants and planners
as is the way of those with no sense or country-manners)
and their keeper Bill McAvish of enlightenment precocious
who held in context his "superiors'" "deeds atrocious"!

Kielder Forest

171

Manitoba 1976 and The Border 1970 (revised 2008)

Under the sun

And darkening when piling cumulus grow and blacken
where the "ringtail" sails along long days' seasons
and short days' seasons, changing tone toward maturity;
furlongs or sections apart there will be other ones,
"blue-hawks", partly-…, the variegated immaturity
for even with these the fulfilments of time will not slacken
where her shadow lengthens with those of the clouds
with the rising sun over the limitless prairie –
where there is prairie left – and at its going down
where hawks and buzzards are too high to cast any;
too few such days and flyings to marvel, never too many…

Black sometimes against the sun, whitening under its glare
just as at home even winter sun can paint the fieldfare
(grey and chestnut in other light) toward black and white
unravel the species in the eyes insufficiently bright
but not, I expect in the clearer, harriers' vision
who follows the flock-stragglers out of the sun
or into it with the same success the same season!

Under aurora

under the green, lightest sphagnum-green, plumes, preen
the coven half-hidden in the bracken
there that night the biggest number I'd seen –
soon after dusk reaching a baker's dozen
hooded in their face-ruffs effigies each
shifting in the stillness, awake at midnight
the moor in front lit up, a silver beach
big yellow full moon behind us and as bright
her willow-leaf spirals, sweeps and sheets follow
spectra of greens and yellows, reds, back to yellow
above and north-face every one, swivelling fellows

Ringtail harrier

she makes no sound; all the sound right for the place
already around, over and under and all around
for those who listen for the river; muffled by the sallows
– the unplanned Salley Gardens; the redpolls in the alders
which seem to be asway on the sicilienne of the willows;
seething of the levels in marshy bits full of the grace:
space she makes yet more graceful by her diffident pace.

'Meeting of the Waters' by Leadgate, Alston Moor
January 14th, 2009

§

"a little of the sky fallen down"
the child said (translated by his mam)
when I showed them blue gled from above;
dunes evenly lit under a "pearly" sky
she said as I helped her with the pram
for the tiring Bryn and the flotsam stuff
their beachcombing morning had 'come by'

cock harrier came back on the track
passing close again, filling our eyes
as she said, like her mascara'd lashes
his black primaries sweeping so low
discreetly, she said 'shyly' along the dune-slack
"what is he looking for?" "Why does he rise
where the dunes are lowest?", "Why flying so slow?"

that bird had heard and continued his turning
"on sixpence" of wind and expanding our yearning –
for which these two would come back and back,
had started something, declared Bryn's frown.

North Wales

as distant, it seemed, just as distant

reluctant as is harrier to show brown bulk or grey
above the horizon, a warning presence to likely prey
they blurred their tuning-fork vibration for half a day –
its heat-haze shimmer before, during, lightlong display
kestrel and harrier working the distance grassley after ley
wheatfield and barley until their green and gold stems play
and picnic teas at the edge of the fields put away!

Brayton Barff as scarcely rises above the Ouse floodplain
distributaries as these hunters again and again
quartered apparently apportioned bounds before the rain
set in evening after evening with its spearing stain
the sun renewed in the mornings of that summer of the gain
to the skies of five harriers – one drowned in a drain –
and no gun came out for them before they were away again…

Vale of York, 1968

§

Outward from poor England the hen harrier's lot improves;
the Uists and Lews of the Hebrides, much elsewhere in Scotland,
everywhere in Ireland, as through France and much of Europe
north of the southern mountain ranges and the med-lands
across the Northern Hemisphere through the temperate Old World and New
if we count in North America's Marsh Hawk range, as I do
and found habits and behaviour similar – even in Alaska…

§

France in schooldays discovering Limousin and the Auvergne
Montagu's and Hen Harriers to distinguish and discern
so very conscious of so very much to begin to learn!
and there began my very bad habit in the minds of 'twitchers'
of standing (or even sitting or lying) still for ages for my riches
able to ignore, with practice, midges', cleggs; mosquitoes' itches.
Not all things come to those who wait, perhaps, but some!

§

'Kyloes' flick their tails like Kyloe Hills under rain-flails
while between grazing monuments darkened ringtail sails
knee-high to head-high amongst them before light fails,
her own flicker-tail guides Till; at home rudders Rotherhope,
nearside burn, open-side pasture-hill, grapples hanging to grope
economical of wind energy, her own, shouldering the break-of-slope.
Summergrowth's wrong movement detected, grasps the frog as cleanly
as in the same long moment she drops him unhurt, so not meanly;
carried, the ball forward in the maul gains ground for me keenly –
not having found frogs here before, as, I'm told, there are no trout…
This reach she's found no vole, mole, no young rabbit caught out,
no big insects or worms for her young. No foolish partridge pullets about.
So she takes a minute to preen in Earthnut, Kecks, and Rattle
and listens to the warning from the rooks' and jackdaws' prattle
and is away and low as crow or fox will go; back through the cattle
– had they 'scented' a gun? There again she twists in the rain
this way and that, hardly rising to the dyke, ducking into the lane
to climb the hill unseen against the sky, somewhere to try again.

North Northumberland 1968

§

to our ears he whispers
"we *are*" through his nostrils
not "we be" like the buzzards
lightly steers fjord or seamarsh
braw enu, twin screws turning
buoyant keel carves our runes
and scrolls larbord to starbord

———————————

centuries later his puff-faced pow
slow-coulters, his pleuf seams grund
contouring for the strips to come now
turned slizers gleam polished sun
yellow his talons, steel claws
blued steel bill modest sickle
for hand-harvesting in scale

———————————

he's flown on regardless through
beside our believed bright waters
and lightening hills, pastures
and after Enclosure, relict moors
hills once remote, now everyone's
to trample, put up off last nest
crush eggs by other agency.

§

*[these the days of the perfume of the 'ling-bonner', I had to go outside
to be dazed by the spring, and little sequence happened...]*

Ahead of the roll of thick smoke over the fell shoulder
far from the nest a raven whom the cloud made bolder
patrolled over a consternation of curlews and peewits
provoking plover complaints – the golden, late-come pipits;
its wind mingled their cries to mournful dissent everywhere.
Spiky rushes shining silver a new distracting glare
unnerving alarms, I expect and prepare for hunters there...

half-a-mile downwind of the billowing roke
its ash-coloured bird hung to and fro like smoke
narrow as a serpent; wavering like one
'dancing' in spring devotedly under the sun;
a strip of flesh pierced and tethered to test
resolve for the sundance vision each make, lest
the hoop of the remnant nation goes unblest

cloudless sun at highest somewhere, penumbra everywhere
spiky rushes shining silver in the eye-tiring glare
all else darkened and merged again as winter's heather stem
a small flight of greylags northward calling soft and unseen
in the mirk apparently more of them than there would have been
harrier lost to sight; I should have 'kept ahead' like him
raven croaking defiance to peewits' outwitting them

Muir-burning near Garrigill, March 19ᵗʰ, 2009

"Marsh Hawk" = Hen Harrier *(Circus cyaneus)*

Satchmo's blues Indiana blown loose   *for Meredith Quatermain*

In the quiet our stilled minds carry
one of his kind lifts, a lot of 'noise'
off abandoned ironworks; to cruise
dihedral aloft over parking-lot, gauge
blues cast on dove-grey plumage
dark wingtips hold the chord, boys
this gleam against gravity in Gary.

Why should blanket-bog so far away
from these greys, in Northumbria and Cumbria
where this one of our rarer birds of prey
prefigures abundance over America
like bittern and osprey? What did you say,
with your husband, visiting Bunting?
"Only the poets arc *really* hunting!"

Gary, Indiana 1973, 2006

§

Northwest moorlands, as of The Long Island's
peatlands and flowe country there as on The Lews
part of the fractured whole of the Scottish Highlands
I find echoed over prairie coteaux, flatts and slews
with their cousin – Marsh Hawks, same *Circus cyaneus*,
Sought 'Blues' and 'Ringtails' there, found them much less rare
even where declared 'absent' – just as on the Manx curraghs…

§

the only puff of wind this rare mid-day
is of its stillness yet of the ringtail under way
past us below our usual break-of-slope
needing beating for buoyancy, to hold slow lope;
we felt the brush intimate across our cheeks
as the gentlest tentative grope; no more power or 'poke'
– we'd come by Norton torque; a bellows-breath of smoke

_____

down there in the burnet and meadow-sweet
leafhoppers stir over ground-hoppers
moving particles attract her attention;
up there the specks of diamond and flecks of white
like stars are watching her from the sun, the gulls
and the haar crosses behind her
low rowing going "oot gang"
where, without the veil and in her own space
her flight, as the humblest wren or pipit
her neighbours, completes with the flourish.

§

Watching the wavy lanky heather they perched on
insecurely – so possibly a nest somewhere near
or that the watcher, fooled, might be lured on…
Then a rabbit or a bird something had skinned
leaving the head on – best breast-meat gone…
Just so we boys treated our kills of game
we would hardly – for shame – take to the house…
Then we'd hear the keening – there *were* young to feed!
and the nest was close upwind. Feel the wind's shear,
calculate, and steer, nothing so easy to find
as ground-nests. But the need to avoid any blame!

§

jack-snipe silently up under my next footstep
trustingly or not, settled down instantly
on cushions, heath-bedstraw in rushes a yard ahead
took me to the dyke looming left as instinctively
for hardly was I as set as the 'bird in buff braces'
(from the pale harness glowing against cryptic brown,
giving the air of an unjacketed brown man-about-town)
when a clatter of kays announced another visitor –
and, on my line, a ringtail came low up the pasture
inches off the ground. The little Snipe ran ahead of her
dodging rush tufts in the way, which may have hidden her.
Large and small brown jockeying nags the jump-races,
had the jacksnipe woodcock eyes in the back of her head?
with a yard start on a zigzag hunting harrier.
On they went, as if playing, a hundred yards at the stagger
and at last I was getting the meaning of 'harrying'
yet didn't see that the ringtail was now 'carrying'
just as she had one of the pullets out of the staggarth

1954, Bilsdale.
kays : jackdaws staggarth : stackyard (Cleveland dialect)

§

We call it beautiful: a steady beat propels the scull
the ship that best left the wave behind her
lest lost amongst gulls and crows and forgetting
the dregs of the storm astern yet
we lose sight of her, cannot grasp the glimpse offered.

But of the hill-mist appears a figure of grace a glance
is all afforded at first against her glides, turns
and she has come by despite all the lazier tracery in the sky
which would take us up – for she flies low, un-noticed,
a single line unfolding over miles.

She has just passed this way on a deliberate progress
not by only quartering for prey has she left
a clear partial track across these acres.
In the reactions, ructions of rushes and sivs
and a score of birds and voles come to attention…

§

for Jeff Radley and Keith Goodway

Right on the beat, as herons also ease and tease
(MacDiarmid agrees) she rides the breeze
that's rocking the droveway's avenue of trees
then picks out ruts for us in the mudstone below.
Jeff challenged me to get this his fine line in
and not just anywhere, but somewhere just so.
"Ye plait of ye auld ways (in Callow)"
slant of light reveals the scars long scored-in
thus the bird unseals for us phytogeography
Keith – species of grasses differ over her quartering
of a temporary but very real geomorphology!

Blue-Hawk: harvest-moon in beginning-gloaming

soon, soon as usual whispers we *are,* not we will be, over the brigg
braw enou turn his twin screw steering near as in fjord, sea
every evening this week seconding the wind aboon you and me
see how between them blusters and whiffles will not let barley-napp ligg!
Larboard to starboard his buoyant keel carves out a curving then closing
      rune
running nowhere but like the loosened boy only for nothing... liking...
      for the moon
transient shadows over depths of feelings score and cut and store barley-bigg!

love that anchored your smallholding against storms warned by Scarth Nick
love that wondered at the blue-hawk' coulter of air above your pleuf:
"he gleams more than molly mauks, yet he seems one of yon now if
a 'Keeper like Thompson is about. So he ignores their every raucous shout
(they don't mob this hawk or the attention they give will bring him down)
"bird of the best hairst could yet clear his ground of stoggies – and quick!"
Ozzy or Potto – wherever he farmed, he pointed stooks toward the Nick.

Out of the horizon came, especially in September when he was most needed;
glances like off steel - never suspecting the 'moor buzzard' was his mate –
  polishing his straw, drawing the yet uncut for rabbits and voles "he weeded
out a few rats an all. Aye, he was worth a few partridge, at any rate."
We'd watched one in the steels and blues whites, of far Northern waters
brightlined like his wings; "dipped deep in Styx. Should be in the Sagas
his quills nonetheless writing in Higgins Ink as if we could pick lines up...

[(his) Cleveland dialect –
ligg: lie; bigg: a form of barley;
pleuf: plough; molly mauks: gulls;
hairst: harvest; stogies: wood pigeons]

For Bill Cowley
1955, 1978

§

head-bobbing as an owl
up on long legs like a burrowing-owl
(don't bury me on this prairie
as you've buried the prairie-dog towns
under cow pasture and concrete)

on the Coteau

scattered downslope

as I passed, and counted seven daughters

silently
each spoke

as the raven always speaks

Missouri Coteau, 1975

West Cut Black Band, Cross Fell)

I chase her lowering the evening sun
(but she stays well ahead of me, and dips under
to chill me.) I keep the ringtail in range but my feet blunder.

She's chased my familiar hare, I think for fun
and teases us both, Harry's old fell, a chorus
of grouse curses cause a rare yelp, counting coup for us

Ignore the struck bird until she has won
distance she can dismiss us from and the game's over
– but she dallies with us, quartering left and right at her leisure…

Regretting it, now why did we bring the gun?
And why hasn't she dropped away off into 'dead ground' or gill?
Night comes on; will she go on hunting or has had her fill?

Two voles enough for the day? Is it done?
she's down at last, but not near the usual roost; not she,
she's (we're near now) picked up another vole, but away she'll flee

At speed now and so low and upsun
(what's left of light) I lose her in the mirk approaching
with the cloud-cloak. Is she joining in my self-reproaching?

Harrier

Whistling as the bird wheels away, the forming ice
closes its lanes in the slack, malice or benediction;
grey of the sky solidifies on its crackling surface
as if the harrier had swept some dark spell over it.
With the next mild blow bubbles show in the cat-ice
and the scene lightens as if to say something from below
like lift of the sea-ice inshore with the tide-race.

———————————

Still caressing the distorting mirror along
she becomes leadline of the edge herself
the estuary begins or ends on her service
harrying for a tarrying wader less strong
and having fed and flown on. At her ossuary
inland in gorse remains accumulate, castings
from her gizzard wheezed up on the same whistling song.

Black Gale, Whale's Eye, Crossfell Range

Yards only ahead of where we stood
wind ahead of the squall shakes cordage
the ferns in the fell-wall, green polypod
nod against snow lining for all mortar;
Harrier just over, ignores us, dove into the wood.

Years before I'd seen the same phenomenon –
a few hundred feet below the black gale, harrier
quartering the ground as if nothing was happening
aloft – rising and falling as if in on a string
in almost a calm, and so patrolled for miles…

She has been perhaps minutes quiet in shelter
perhaps assessing the winds, or gathering *her* strength
we saw her catch nothing that afternoon, at length.

The gale, they say, gusted a hundred that day
the Dun Fell instruments "were helter-skelter."
Blast through the cols which between the summits lay
tumbles us over easier than the Helm wind had,
No other bird stirred. Business must have been bad?!

§

Face split double to see binocularly
he harrows the fells like their seams of gripps
a stone axe slipping its gleam and harmlessly
side to side as she prefaces simple pleughs
coulters and turns attention seamlessly

§

Of course, as you'd expect, from the northwest

    a purple ship-cloud, ahead of the rest
    and the great black bank of coming snow
    hung like a flag low down over the crest
    toward where I had waited for whatever would show

she doesn't neglect the blue-back beetle
indigo-edged of spectrum from scurrying
I find shards of their elytra scattered about
from the breakdown of her regurgitated castings
around her nest-site and again at her roost
– exhibiting the same preference through the seasons
for what is not the commonest species at either…

    she who makes the windless sloughgrass
    ripple as if a badger or rabbit tried to pass
    through the stems; so close above she flew
    put my mind sideways to those North Sea tideways
    when the gannets seem to know precisely what's below
    before they dive for fish from height; quick aim not astray.
    Above her, reverse of shadow, wheeled and pried
    mocking yes flocking nearer if something had died
    the raven of the place waited-on for her prey
    – two percent of hunts, can he take it away
    for watchers, raven and me, 'Ken' grows so slow…

    it is more convenient for the message
    that these are as out of sight, or 'extinct'
    or unlikely as the rarest bird-of-passage
    the 'twitchers' flock to. We are not to *think*
    but know only 'expectation' as Consumers
    and believe the 'experts', willy-nilly;
    whose vested-interest (They are the exhumers
    of the New Reality, academic 'IN' air, of secrecy…
    archaeologists of what-was, and not what is.

§

The ringtail carried the plover a few hundred yards to a prominent place on the raised-bog and began to pluck rather awkwardly until a rather loud "peek, peek" (well-repeated) call some way off recalled last week's kite and sure enough there 'it' (surely there's only one) flew in from the ghyll direction as if to join in the feed. A kerfuffle at that distance. Light not good enough to be sure no tags or dye. Both big birds in the air over the corpse, though, an effortful thrash of rings and bangles.

The red kite broke off, only a few feathers had been lost by either or both birds, and flew low round the darkness of Burnhope Seat in Teesdale, the harrier at the plover immediately and took less than ten minutes (leaving a scraggy mess sans breast, sans head, hardly plucked, drumsticks stripped roughly and jerked 20 feet away. Black redstart calling late this afternoon from just above the village; otherwise little passerine activity bar dippers – one singing from Ashgill and two at the ford near the redstarts' centre-of-gravity (and their nest-site, two years now).

Spent the middle part of the day indoors and writing; had Mary Gill visit with a "bachelor's" Christmas pudding, and one for Dennis, who was also on the fell this morning and has seen a, or the, ring-tail apparently trying to get close to about 40 fieldfares feeding on the ground (crowberries).

November 25th, 2002

Ranging

we gauge the depth of peat with the auger-poles
marked off in feet. Then the theodolite
to determine direction of flow from the surface below
these glacial-overflow channels. But so
much easier the harriers tell me the right
grain of the land by flying in for their voles
geometer also by the plants and the runs of the moles!

§

The high plateau where curlew and skylarks rise
over the 'blanket bogland' not to be despised;
as other deserts, these have their abundance:
seasonal Chevron, Antler, Fox Moths, Eggars,
Craneflies in heavy cops; each once fat larva;
beetles and spiders; metal to soft substance!
On each of these and more, harrier gorges
especially when young – so much in reach
where the moss, the bracken, the heather merges
the bents and rushes and bog-flower flushes
trickles off peat-hags also nourishing chicks
of the wading birds parents have had to learn tricks
to catch by ruse, surprise, mainly on the ground
where we hardly see them, even moving around!

Border Forests, English Side

Spruce planted
new opportunity

before these aliens'
maturing uniformity.

Chez* sez
he planted millions
at piece rates
made hundred of pounds,*
Displaced person
replaced harriers

Dave knew where they nested
year after year showed me
but the closed forest denied
them and their hunting.

(It is some effort to stand amongst them.)

(1978)

* 'Chez', Pole ex-8th Army,
features in *Poems In North Tynedale*.

(Urra, 1960)

When she circles round the round-barrows
the burial-mounds high on our moors
dating back to the Bronze Age at least
in constellations spread open to the east
a hoop of the people is complete
even if not comprehended. Feet
are encouraged to follow hollow
ways still traced, if you can swallow
"old trods" and birds' elusive spoor...

§

"as if" he said "this *was* a 'Nant' in Wales"
we marvelled at the sight from High Rampgill Mine
of the Romans' Whitley 'Castle', built for oversight
of their lead mines – no doubt worked by native slaves –
along the valley of the Nent river, his "sight so fine"
with that harrier plying the bents on the wind, left to right
almost under our noses "but is she foolish or all right
flying so close to us!" Thus Roy Currie, chest fit to bust*
from our exertion up the fell, "agh, the scales
had come off" his eyes in surprise but "aye, what ails
her?" I thought, maybe the holy 'disease' of trust...

*He died suddenly, prematurely, a 'mole' – expert enthusiast
of mines history ('nent, nant', old Welsh – once the language of
Cumbria – for 'valley')

191

Harrier and Snow Owl

Hanging on the onshore wind now the norwester squall dies
to dry, or prospecting for meadow-vole runs and lies
drab at our distance, tatterdemalion ringtail
apparently casually tacks back to glide and sail
all canvas on, gaining safe height overhead and away
a little after dawn on that rare rarebird sort of day
Blezard had advised us on; Armstrong hero met in a blizzard
Armstrong Marley and me, visitors from over the Pennines
hanging on every word ('as Bramwell Evens'), wanting hazard…

sunk in himself stumps about, grumpy umpire giving the score
faces the wind, as meek charadriform on the shore
shape-shifter; a loose bag of blowing snowy feather
pillow with its cover worn away in places by weather
shadow awry, fleece shorn in parts only by rough nature
and season, not by shears and schedule, stuffed caricature
of the neat shape in the illustrations, yet he shakes wings
folding their triple planes, extending covert-tracts over
combing in the wind face – muff from deep dark glug-hole eyes
allowing no close approach before he extends all   to rise
over the same old wildfowler who'd shown me short-eared owls
hunts with the shorteared slowly for the Solway South shore
– with the peregrine patrolling above, beware all smaller fowls!
For us, though we don't know it yet, yet more fragments in store.

'Back o' Skiddaw' 1957,
revised 2009

by RA1388 on Otterburn Ranges

We've come as near as we can by the road
laid-down for tanks, motorised artillery.
What is that flag or flak exploding in air – my goad
but the dihedral of blue-hawk air-mastery?

_____

there up the fellside, only the sounds say Spring;
I sweep the horizons despite bewildering
distracting exulting peewits' bickering
so sweetly all around me, wingclaps sting ears
fearsomely close whilst the 'ringtail' slowly steers
sweeping this way through sleety spears
a wet week before the laverock would sing.

_____

of 1926 '6-80' Brough Superior
half-an-hour after the run is still 'pinging' slow
cast-iron barrels, cast-alloy crankcases inset
attracting the attention of the camp's gunnery officer
(I'm glad he hadn't heard her rattle under valve-caps!
coming over Ottercops) pleased to see the harriers:
"1388 the date of the Battle, sir; don't you know?"

§

it seems someone else's boyhood now:
Arken beck and Arden*, Scarth Nick and Birk Brow,
the Pendle Hill I learned to walk on, on heather, on fell
cushioned with sprung steps on tussocks as well, –
Bollands Fells smooth at my elbow, lovely nurse
humming and dancing her bumble-bees' strung verse
needing only hearing over not to be forgotten –
nor the birds of prey about, *making* every day
stronger than song, buzzard above, kestrel below
and merlin and harrier interrupting the pipits to show
how after them for the rest of my life I'd have to stray

* *that by Snilesworth, Hawnby*

§

looking for him many an empty road and mile of space
gulls look like him, many other birds' resemble his grace
but not quite; only with time you'll know what's right is right
is then right. The mind clears through hours of day and night
thousands of hours "no-one in his own mind"... And his mind
beyond our reckoning, yet beckoning some to find
chance special in the 'yowe-trummel', be ready to perceive
(looking is not seeing), a sceptic head, heart to receive
by discipline of diagnostic features to believe...

there he is, at bramble fruit hanging as for benefit
of you as he is, as he has turned aside just for it
the trivial, the dessert, perhaps to aid digestion
after a surfeit of voles swallowed whole, their congestion
of grass seed and grass cuttings, avens' husks, mosses' capsules
– to nail down this hunter, hunter, adjust your graticules
dismiss the platitudes; – the reality; – his castings
(and only *partial* evidence). And the watchings lasting
lifetimes of world wide naturalists ignored by 'science'...

Hunderthwaite

At a mile her shallow vee in the sky steered toward,
where we, in cover, had recognised her as a 'Ring-tail'...
She overflew up to have a close enough look, at over a hundred paces;
clearly she carried a woodcock to no great loss of her graces.
I'm captive, to how she caressed against the wind each rushes' rank
to tell the marvel one day of how she glides each bank
and swell with the tussock-grass and heather clumps rhythm
to dwell over cotton-grass upwards from its within;
its blanket-bog rise after rise, this upland's last stell
falls behind in neglect as she climbs broad Mickle Fell
by its long leg, westward, which we call The Boot.
The bird keeps out of range, he's no chance to shoot,
friend 'keeper, kindly John Parkinson Of the Gurt Thirst;
she's away, and of course we are tiring first.

(for my mother –
Walking Stainmore by Brough to Bowes to meet her where the Greta descends,
cutting its curtsey 'bows' deep I bowed greeting to the Icelandic river Griota
two years ago – theirs is as 'stony' but its banks are not so steep!)
1957; revised 2007

Circus cyaneus ('Ring-tail') Hen Harrier

leggy as the leaning ling
low over these high grouse-grounds
'*circus*' implies her circuits –
rounds around sphagnum mounds
circles hummocks in sequence
(grouse long gone from her presence
she seeks the mere creeping
thing; the vole, the lizard, mouse...)

Wind Mountains, Wyoming

Wind down this side, their lee,
today for their hay I've asked to be,
out of where storms breed...

Less confined that they
comes this 'gleed' to prey
(and 'after the manner of ploughing a field';
as people here say
"in a holy way"
where ancestors and he have set their seed)
– asking ground-squirrels to yield.

1973, 1975

§

switchback display, advertisement equivalent to song
but are these blue-hawks competing against one another
or otherwise stimulated, do they display as long
here where are several territories 'circumjacent'?

and they display before there are ringtails in evidence
but do the ringtail females assess, compare the males
by the territories indicated by these displays? –
they must have an eye for country from hunting experience

not so ephemeral for us, and surely so for them –
we feel the sky dance vibrations in the air; our bodies
react with our voices; pulsing on that high excitement!

1970s
'Bolland' with Everard Flintoff

§

Cock hen-harrier takes the brightest cock
from the little "mealies" feeding-flock
(maybe only one family) I'm
under instruction to shoot or lime
for The Collection, by St. Abb's Head;
I might have prevented that capture
striking first, to a lesser rapture!

1962

§

[for those with me who have watched for Science,
whether they knew it then or not. Opt for grace]

Fortieth year of harrier wintering-places
generation after generation we seek increase

'Harrier Notes' reduce to a fraction
or increase to one; compare any fractal

what cannot be reduced or increased, the factual
from disciplined observation and its repetition

reluctant unfurling, inward toward theory
outward, as the harrier prospects, to notion

curiosity will not grant its own, any, cease
or even easing-up. 'Office hours' a negation

as of life and truth, if we speak so bold.
The harrier quarters-on heedless, noticing.

Inward or outward, we may see as this one
widdershins or shadowed, wet, cloud, snow or sun.

1995

Above a burn's springs, scanning

The line of rushes lengthens by a presence
palpable and not flapping in the breezes
military-medium their wavings straggle
steadily santering, it is extending their cover
by himself or herself, identity as if with theirs
deliberate as a cat stalks but the lifted hairs
are feathers brushed above spindleshanks, a waggle
tail toggled on at the rear end; cobbled-up, easing.
Hunched hag, not a heron's concentration
hours as minutes as fruitless in his essence.
Yet I was prevented going-on, going up there
winter-god had shaken the bridge at Langleeford
in spate of spite itself strong enough to hold rare
awareness I couldn't express. The latent harrier.

1976

§

in a shimmer off the reservoir, glimmer
of "liberty under discipline"
agreed Bessie and Granny that summer.
Change of tone with the tide of the spate
arriving from a hundred sikes and becks:
"liberty needed now to fight spite and hate!"
ringtail shot on the nest in the kecks
and not even taken away – is that shame
or liberty of soul? In the game
the dangerous game of dominion
there must be space for mercy's opinion

§

We stopped for sandwiches "aboon the muckle toon"
impatiently at that, for just over the hill
the family I'd hopes to show her, tho' not so soon,
were also and as delicately, having *their* fill…*
We came upon them immediately on our resumption
as if at cricket, after the interval for luncheon
a hot day we could have been even more lazy.
They've been here since he as a child on the "Mazy
Snake" of the Border waters, Hugh MacDiarmid
who delighted in his old age to hear me tell of them
even as we watched a harrier over there at Biggar
"their sleights of hand marvellous in the glide
I remember". And their stamina, persistence, vigour
every man's hand against them, and they canna hide…
As a boy, like Bunting and I in our time
drawn to Tarrasdale's silence of secret place
just as the birds were, when they were allowed space
and *none* of us can catch their grace in rhyme!

*in previous years there, of grouse and wader chicks, adult pipits and other small
birds, lizards and frogs and large insects, and (in a good vole year) over a hundred
short-tailed voles…*

For Margaret, Yorkshire Cricket Club…

(Immature harrier takes up residence)

Coming-on again in search of what was lost yesterday here
gold ring from her eye, blued gun-metal of talon and of cere,
yellow, unexplained brightness of shanks and toes' authority
of executive rank; yet she exhibits caution, temerity
using the height of dyke, hang of peat haggs, wind-waves in bracken
and ling clinging to the slopes in brakes; awaits wind slacken
gliding so low, inspecting everything by slight turns of head
ahead by minute correcting adjustments of rudders; a 'gled'
indeed, even along the gripps I use to hide myself
a full furlong from her plucking-place gritstone shelf.
Sheer intensity, dead reckoning gives each our wealth.

*

An hour's spate will show, tell us how, not why,
when the Big Blackfoot roared and rolled
reach after reach, steep woods, narrow beach
along its long canyon; Marsh Hawk's road
seeks to hide him, blue between water and sky
flies after surprised sandpiper, calling cold,
told the moment: splashed stone can teach –
dry in an hour. Ploated on that boulder
of only main feathers and then swallowed whole.

Montana
1973, 1976, 1996, 1997

Towering

At height there is one towering bird
now the sky is clear of peregrine and raven
at intervals across the sky a second and a third
rise with the May thermals over the swidden
each own style to spiral tension of spring
each rising and falling as if on a string

Nearest, the jack merlin, regardless of the laverock
a hundred yards on and his natural prey
more aware of his partner jill merlin on her rock
lookout where the Yoredales break the surface grey
(preening carelessly, or so it seems to me)

But further off is the performance of the morning
a furlong away perspective; a furlong in height
the blue hawk speck a black midge against awning
milk white and blue, and he, dropping, is the might
of Thor's hammer – he must smash against the hill!
but pulls out of the dive as fast as a peregrine will
not for the kill but to his mate on the ground stockstill!

§

Sweeping low across level haughlands
lifting-up terraced beveled pastures
seeming leisurely following Tyne's bendings
rabbit-lawns, longmeadow dykes' wendings
'leading nowhere' whereas this bird is going
steadily somewhere, not a random flowing
no more than the river's meanders.
Your delight in your "busard de St. Martin"
(our Hen Harrier) progressing by starting
-up partridges all the way to Snabdaugh*
before breakfast the day "already enough!"

*pronounced "snabduff"
1982
With F.N Genty, Greystead

§

Widdershins is her quartering now
something suggests her diurnal round
a backspin-trajectory of Earth
when I plot her ellipses of haugh*

Seasonal shift in this tendency
– almost a rule – is it strategy
or the progression of depressions
in from the Atlantic – energy
she uses, choosing some directions?
Coincides with the better 'vole years',
when she hunts most when the linestorm stirs.

* pronounced "haff", or "hoff", or "horf"...

§

Watched a ringtail slowly up from the dale
ignored by the cuckoo searching the heather
scotching "itchygrubs" of Fox Moth, Northern Eggar
and maybe Emperor Moth and, on a smaller scale,
this hill's own special of Tiger moths' caterpillars
successful until, by the bubbling call, this female
gowk gave the game away and the big harrier
choked the cheer as the dwindle at a cistern's filling
grasping with both feet, dropping on her from behind
efficient as a terrier at a rat, more chilling
as there are few enough cuckoos now, but thrilling to mind!…

Yad Moss, July 1993

§

because the underground swam out of the ground
as she swims out of the breaks of slope all around
where mineworkings have been and the outcroppings
and she hunted the swalleys for their sheltering snipe
and these moss-creeperpipits which fell into their gripe
she earned her legend from our surprise and heartstoppings
over the sodden pastures raising a little mist of her own
sudden as slink fox stink on these well-keepered fells
 the same sense, for where she has not grown

She is above it all yet her wings darken in the wet
one heavier, leading wing a rowing oar like the scow
steering keel boats or the Missouri flatboats, as slow
tacking a progress close to the wind or the current set
under the wind from landscape's fret

§

If we want the day-fill
ringing the louder for seeming soundless
against wind and hill
eyes opened and closed long after this
and she flies, quartering still.
As music is from noise by repetition
gaudies' quarter-mile alarm attention
silences mine but strengthens her will;
patience lengthens to her eventual kill
birdsong resuming after suspension
is only the passed-over dunlin's trill.

Crookburn 1986

§

Like shite shines after eel-meal tells
of little black red eels out of the peatpools
not the big brown serpents of Trenholme stell
– meatier than Petch's pies today, you fools!

———————

She watches lanky heron cranking up, trailing slime
heaves up a frog too many, this spawning-time
and takes his place on a post to watch the water
takes my first water-rail, lets me escort her
to another post to pluck, ploat, the quiet crake
discard all but the breast on its bone and make
it crack, split shield, with a heron-like croak.

Cleveland, 1961

Where Rise Watters of Tyne, Tees, Wear

The ringtail no longer visible
has merged into the winter brown
wingstroke by wingstroke down
under the sky, into the deceivable

———————————

Using the spillway channel left over
from the great ice melt not so long ago
when we consider pedigree of this rover
know more than the genome will show

———————————

Off the spiky blanket-bog peatlands spread
for the smallest falcon as for our rare gled
where becks rise from and burns are born
and so the Three Rivers some southrons scorn…

———————————

Let hawks hold the upland, 'empty' or 'bare'
and let us guard *their* territory up there
from 'playground' development, F.W.D.'s
– there's more than human greed to please…

Cock Hen Harrier

Watch and ward through to horizon's black fell barrier
he moves along the ridges part of their grey vapours
sometimes with brighter crest or light linings below
white underwing and underflanks of this harrier
seeming only a little more solid, and quite as slow
drifting with the thin wind within its dismal lift
briefly enlivening that gap far fells show through
sky and moor his whole life-ground weld and rift.
At last light offers, opens, his promised hint of blue.

Hen Hen Harrier

Circus cyaneus, female, on course at shallow dihedral angles
circuits tortuous as the moss *Tortella tortuosa* tangles
on this blanket-bog, self edged of sedges, grasses coarser and finer —
margins eroded by our track over, follower the former miner;
she where his channels lead along contours to where his hushes
cut the fellside to show him the veins and she in the cover of rushes
the voles she manoeuvres for by her head's and her talons' dangles.

(*Circus cyaneus* L. scientific name for the Hen Harrier)

§

They say I go for the 'rarities' like a trophy-hunter, and I dare
because despite some "experts'" pronouncements there are some there,
if they believed, and got off their backsides, they could share!
Ah, the individual, no matter how 'common' or how 'rare'
we must employ the 'population' sense of Ernst Mayr;
there is no standard indexed identity only each 'isness'
as for each of us, if we have a natural awareness

§

yes, its an 'arrête', but it's not dangerous yet
but it's caused you to miss the big paleblue
course undeflected, for he is true to the land's
lie, all his hinterland subtended by this fell
and is almost alone in it and all this winter,
hundreds of square miles to hunt its red grouse
if he had that skill; otherwise rabbits and voles!

aye, he's arresting; the day dulls after he's gone
and I regret the great drifts kept a sight of him
from you up these long snow slopes from below
but he may come over twice and give another chance
and all we usually are afforded of his like anyway
is the peculiar glimpse or glance at his passing
greys or silver-blues fine as snow's reflections

this late in winter, but with lambing-storms to come
he may not indicate yet territory and a nest
(but so it proved that year, one the RSPB missed
and a far hill-farmer was privileged to find)
yet something in his buoyancy and dwell
might suggest he is at home, as we are near ours
and, as you say, it is hope that feeds the mind!

A Blues For Wannies (two views)

SPRING

A nest of harriers on the Wannies in the 'sixties
indicates a few of their richnesses, intricacies;
a season when there were no blue peregrines
and only a single pair of brown air-blue merlins.
The blue hawk arrived early, early as February
and displayed late March; though remaining wary
with apparently little of the sky-diving extravagance
or maybe his intended was looking blue or askance!
The nest itself, midden and green decoration, unlocks
the Alpine richness of so-called 'base-rich' rocks
having twists of vernal grasses and of bright *polytrichum*
eggs laid on rushmat, twirls of red and white sphagnum.

SUMMER

...and have successfully already, though voles are now few,
grown up when the moor-grass turns blue
from glaucous-seeming to me the same variety
I find abundant in Upper Teesdale – Harwood, and see
but less often, on Westmorland Fells away from the limestone
where it is common. Surely such ground is best for the bone
of the long limbs and body of these fine fledglings clowning
to gain strength even as their tidying plumages are browning
as if in the sun. The young are all to be henbirds, but one
the 'runt' – amongst five bullies he isn't having much fun...!

Postscript

Bringing-together these pieces to some sort of assembly
in October 2008, I am sent a typical example of
present-day media-opinion -– the *Daily Telegraph*'s – under the
heading "Britain's rarest bird of prey not recovering",
thus; "Hen Harrier numbers are showing no signs of recovery
in England, conservationists warned yesterday… chicks were successfully
reared in just 10 nests, out of 19 attempts. Last year there were
14 successes from 23 attempts." Of course, 'grouse moor managers'
got the blame for this. An RSPB spokesman; "If there is no illegal
killing, as some grouse-shooting interests would have us believe, then
where are the missing birds?" Responses arise from my experience, and
no doubt others' (quite apart from the nonsense of the hen harrier as the
"rarest bird of prey" in Britain; even if 'breeding' is inferred, what about the
sea eagle, eagle owl, snowy owl, and quite a few other candidates?)
My own observations alone, and for the 5 Northernmost counties of
England alone for the two successive years give successful nests rather more
numerous than the RSPB figures. I get tired of trying to point out that the
RSPB information is partial (in both senses…) and their 'missing birds'
    are about…

27th October 2012 colder, not overcast and cold NNW breeze

First light this morning above Tynehead; a light hill mist scarfing slight snow spatters from overnight; that patchiness from say 1700' up; light wind from the north northwest; and a pale harrier in the distance at Meadowhead was perched above several blackgame feeding near the South Tyne on the rough ground below the waterfall on the South slopes, rushy ground. The harrier rose for the meadowland ruins to fly slowly into the remains of the hill mist and out of sight. The blackgame had taken no notice, but red grouse alarmed over the nearer part of my 'study area' for a few moments only.

Patrick Vercrambre and then Tom Pickard called on me mid-morning and we drank coffee and chatted, not of the birds, before Tom and I went to Alston for a little shopping and watched a male buzzard mobbed by jackdaws above Redwing.

When Tom and I got back to Cross Fell Cottage with the porridge oats I noticed a movement along the fell adjacent, northwards, at distances less than a hundred yards to about half a mile away of steadily rising-and-falling moderate bunches, more or less loose, of redwings; many calling. Against the wind, NNW about 3-4mph, they dipped and dithered, the sort of flight I'm used to seeing small flocks of them prospect for berries, especially the ground berries – many 'parcels' of birds were only a few yards high, and most were below the tops of the sycamore clump at the top of the first rise of the fell – at about 450'. The movement seemed to have just started; we had come via Leadgate and would have met any early parties except when they might have been hidden by the discontinuous village 'street'. I counted and estimated 1400 birds in about 18 minutes and there were further parties after Tom had left – to another 400 or so and stragglers singly and as twos and threes until the whole hour had passed and over 1800 birds had moved through: being watched out of sight for the later 20 minutes or so. Before Tom left we had celebrated this spectacle and I pointed out a harrier at about 7 o'clock behind the main party, of about 450 birds, flying low and pitching briefly on or (to the birds) behind dykes, keeping their speed and about 50-80 yards away in a tangential direction.

Following up the later larger groups on foot via the first limb of the Cross Fell track and the fell side of the 'top' dyke (i.e. at about 1450') I had the harrier dogging them like a submarine after a convoy and surely they were aware of him (a subadult male hen harrier, bold now in weak sunlight) onto Robert Bell's 'allotments' – the great procession could be seen to over 2 miles ahead and level – continuing past High Dryburn House. I'd lost the harrier and thought it had used dead ground to get 'above' me but it suddenly appeared at speed out of Dryburn bottom, sparrowhawk fashion 'jumping' the cross dykes and engaging a party of six or seven redwing rather detached from the rest and about 50' short of the tail of the party, which was over my head and to my right side; all still at about 6 mph – several parties had deviated somewhat but returned to the general flight line as if to allow me to catch up and most parties had at least 1 or 2 vocalising gently (the characteristic flight-note in what I call the Icelandic jargon). The blue hawk had grasped one bird quickly by a loop, and dropped. I was very tired by now but did find the harrier feeding, a flurry of feathers almost reaching me, for 20 minutes (to well after 2pm). I got back soon enough, thrilled, and found 'the Ellot'* 'waiting' for me near home.

(*Elliot Ridley, hill farmer c 75 y.o. with news of other birds)

Lightning Source UK Ltd.
Milton Keynes UK
UKOW04f1832070415

249248UK00001B/22/P